1001 Sci-fi Writing Prompts

Prompts

That will motivate you creatively

- -

CHRISTINA ESCAMILLA

INTRODUCTION

Dear Reader,

It is my hope you will find these prompts stimulating enough to help you with short stories, plays, poems, and even full length novels. When you read a prompt, feel free to expand upon it or use it directly as a plot point.

Science fiction, in its most basic form, is all about exploration. One cannot overlook the "science" of it all. It speaks to that inherent part of us that wants to keep discovering more about ourselves and the world around us. When I was a child, some of my fondest memories were watching science shows with my dad. I was fascinated by the fact that the known world was just a small fraction compared to the unknown. It was that love of science and the idea of infinite knowledge that led me to sci-fi.

Science fiction may not be completely grounded in reality, but it has the same ideology. It takes theory and the unknown and merges them. Whether this is through the inclusion of aliens or zombies, sci-fi speaks to the explorer in all of us. It may overlap on a lot of different genres, such as horror or fantasy, but that same initial basis is the same.

So when you use these prompts, expand your mind and think outside the box. These prompts are like your fuel, but the pumps, nozzle, and guidance system are your rocket, and it can only come from you.

Now go out and touch the stars!

Happy Writing,

Christina

How to Use This Book

I segmented the most common science fiction themes to make for easier reading. However, keep in mind that many elements tend to overlap. For example, it wouldn't be uncommon to have a story that deals with both androids and genetic engineering. In addition, science fiction can be categorized as hard or soft, depending on the level of "realness" of the science (soft being lax, and hard needing a great deal of realistic qualities).

Science fiction also bleeds easily into other genres. For example, an alien story might fit nicely with horror, while a space opera might be akin to a romance. There is no rule that says you must fit your story neatly inside a box. With that in mind, I tried to offer a diverse collection that offers you a great deal to work with. You will find some overlap in these prompts as well. Moreover, the prompts were either drawn from real life facts and occurrences, or straight from the fabrics of my imagination.

Not only is each theme placed into parts, but rather than using open ended questions, I simply offered a catalyst for a story. For this reason, I used words such as "unnamed character" or "protagonist" and many gender neutral terms. The key is to build *your* story around these ideas, including your own unique characters.

Best of luck!

Table of Contents

Aliens, Otherworldly Visitors, & UFOS

Here's something many people might find a little surprising about me—I have an irrational fear of aliens. Although this fear is grounded in the unknown, it's also largely about their intent. *What do they want? Why are they here?* It's these questions that have plagued mankind since they first held an eye to the stars. Of course, if you are familiar with the Fermi paradox, then you know visitors from the stars might be an outright impossibility. However, there are still schools of thought that continue to lead us to beg the question: *Are we alone?*

First Contact

First contact refers to the first time humans become aware of aliens, whether it is on a neutral, aggressive, or passive basis. In most popular science fiction, Hynek's six classification scale is often used:

- 1st **Contact**: UFO seen less than 500 feet away.
- 2nd **Contact**: UFO with physical effect is observed. (For example, electronics stop working).
- 3rd **Contact**: UFO contact with observable sentient pilot or intelligent communication is conducted.
- 4th **Contact**: Alien abduction occurs.
- 5th **Contact**: Direct intelligent communication.
- 6th **Contact**: Death of human or animals caused by aliens.
- 7th **Contact**: Alien/Human hybrid is created.

In this section, we will only deal with 1 – 3 forms of contact.

Later, we'll play with the other forms of contact. For now, let's see what those aliens want, shall we?

1.   *It started with the internet. At once, the world's population of email users are greeted with the same message. At first, it seems like a hoax, an elaborate one, but then everything takes a turn for the worse. Afterwards, everyone points fingers at terrorists, but the truth quickly comes out.*

2.   *They were looking at the sky when they should have been looking at the sea. It begins with a change in the migration patterns of commonly followed species. Then, as more odd changes occur, scientists begin to investigate. They find strange underwater recordings they can't explain.*

3.   *According to many schools of thought, as well as most popular science fiction, if aliens exist then they are most likely to have certain genetic traits. They would have bilateral symmetry, forward facing eyes, and, essentially, a lot of reasons why they might look just like us. Crush that theory. These aliens look nothing like us, and that makes communication very difficult.*

4.   *It was all because of peanut butter. After a heavy rainstorm, and with no power to heat food, an unnamed character decides to dig into the hardly used pantry for a would-be delicious PB&J. There, they find a very scared, very alone creature not from this world.*

5.   *While travelling along a dark road one night, an unnamed character's engine suddenly dies. Baffled, they get out of the car to investigate. Above them, they see a star shining a*

little brighter than the others. Gradually, the star gets brighter and brighter until it touches down where this character is standing. Out of the light steps a strange figure. They whisper, "I know the secret of the universe."

6. *One sunny day, an unnamed character runs across an unusual family. One member wears a moleskin coat with basketball shorts, another is dressed in a full length pink ball gown, and another has on a thick fur coat despite the hot temperatures. There are even two little ones waddling around in duck costumes. The one in the moleskin coat sticks out their hand and says, "Hello, fellow Earthling. Can you point me in the direction of the King?"*

7. *An unnamed character arrives at a recycling bin to get a couple of bucks for their cans. While waiting for the lot manager, something whizzes by their head. Then something else and something else. Suddenly, object after object fly past, all made of metal. When the keys fly out of their hand, they debate whether or not to follow them to see where they are going.*

8. *Two unnamed characters are hiking through the woods. While deep in conversation, they find themselves in an area they have never been before. Sticking out of the bushes is a piece of glinting metal. It's a door. Curious, they open it and find a winding staircase that leads down, down, down. At the bottom, they decide to continue onward until they reach an alien statue with crystal eyes. Light begins to shine*

from them. Little do they know, it's a beacon, calling to
another world.

9. *At once, every known radio frequency on the planet begins*
    to filter out the sound of smooth jazz. Although the sound is
    quite pleasant to many, no one knows what to make of it.
    That is, until the sound is followed by a strange message
    from a distant world.

10. *In 1962, a radio message was sent in Morse code to the*
    planet Venus from the Evpatoria Planetary Radar. The
    messaged contained the words "MIR", "SSSR", and
    "LENNIN". Known as "the Morse Message", no one ever
    expected to hear back. Until one day it happened.

11. *While on a space station, a lonely astronaut looks outside*
    the window, quietly positioned inside the Cupola. The
    unnamed character watches the planet while thinking of
    their life back home. Then something draws them out of
    their thoughts. Through squinted eyes, they see it's a
    spaceship like they've never seen before. And it's getting
    closer.

12. *You've silently watched the Earth on this side of the*
    universe for quite some time. Now your superiors want you
    to make contact. Contact with Earthlings? The job seems
    simple enough, but you aren't sure if you're up to the task.

13. *Long ago, when the Earth was young, there lived a small*
    group of Homo sapiens who had just stepped off the
    evolutionary branch with the discovery of created light—
    fire. This discovery created warmth, turned raw food into

something with less bacteria, and scared away would-be predators. It also became a signifying light that said mankind was ready to receive a message that would kick start the next stage in knowledge.

14. *In the middle of Roswell, New Mexico, a local bar is having "Dress Like an Alien Night". The costumes are great! Some are opting to go as one of the Grey's, a few are donned in green from head to toe, and one is wearing two feet of prosthetics, which is sure to be a crowd favorite. Then a stranger comes in wearing no costume at all. They do, however, have some strange markings on their arms. They sit at the barstool and ask for "as much water as you got".*

15. *In this scenario, first contact occurs through an open letter of sorts. One day every television, radio, internet stream, and so forth showcase the same message in all known languages: "We come in peace." Almost everyone thinks it's a joke, a bad one, but that's when they show up.*

16. *While investigating a murder, a detective stumbles across a body that is unusual. It is in some type of cryogenic state. As the investigator tries to make sense of everything, they hear the sound of footfalls behind them. They turn around, but it's too late. The alien attacks first.*

17. *The otherworldly visitors have been watching for quite some time. In fact, there are certain members whose sole job is to track a human from infancy to death— approximately 80 to 100 years. The only rule for these*

watchers is to never make contact. But one visitor becomes
infatuated with their charge and reaches out.

18. *The major speculation for many first contact tales is that it*
will be done through direct means facilitated by the aliens
themselves. Perhaps, however, first contact is made
indirectly, through a non-dominate species that lives on the
alien planet. Maybe they reached out for help to overthrow
their alien overlords, or maybe they simply made a
mistake.

19. *Playing again with the idea of indirect contact. Perhaps*
members of two different planets are communicating with
each other. The messages can contain a number of different
things, but what happens to them bears the most
importance. A human spacecraft accidently picks up the
messages and then, believing it was meant for Earth, acts
upon it.

20. *In theoretical science, there are many hypotheses that*
involve more dimensions than we are accustomed to. One
of the foremost theories is that these dimensions parallel
one another. Perhaps this is one of the ways interstellar
travel is possible, though it's not through a spacecraft, but
one's body. One day an unnamed character is minding
their own business when suddenly they feel a jolt, followed
by a series of vibrations. Then, clear as day, a voice in their
head—perfectly understandable despite the language
barrier--asks what planet this is.

21. *UFOs come in many shapes and sizes, from rounded dirigibles to modern flying saucers. In this scenario, none of these objects are used. Instead, aliens visit the planet through matter that is akin to clouds. An unnamed character, while enjoying a sunny day and describing what animals the clouds look like, is startled when a booming voice comes from one of them.*

22. *Many people suspect crop circles are nothing but hoaxes. In fact, it's been proven how easily they can be recreated. But what if they are not hoaxes? What if the same message has been repeated century after century in many different "words", desperately hoping to gain our attention?*

23. *There is so much speculation of a military cover-up involving aliens that a whole collection of novels could be filled with how far the conspiracy goes. In this scenario, suppose the story only involves one report from a government document revolving around the first time contact with beings from another planet is made.*

24. *One of the more popular "ancient alien" theories is that the pyramids were built as a type of beacon to other worlds. Perhaps this is true and one hot day, while slaves are working and the dynasty is in full swing, the Egyptians finally get an answer back.*

25. *Communication doesn't happen with words and it doesn't happen through hand motions. Instead, communication is done through complex math problems that are sent over interstellar communications. No one is quite sure what this*

alien message is saying until one day an unnamed character cracks the code.

26. *An unnamed character has had enough of loneliness and decides to post an ad on a popular website. They use the normal acronym to describe themselves (ex. SBM or SWW, etc.). Curiously, one respondent replies with SNH. As it turns out, the NH stands for "non human".*

27. *First contact is made by a hapless child who stumbles across an alien visitor while walking home from school. Assuming this child has some kind of weight over the world, the visitor instantly makes their demands and refuses to negotiate with anyone else.*

28. *It begins with a loud bang that shakes the inside of a submarine. The gathered scientists—on a mission to explore the depths of the oceans--have come across an ancient ship. By appearance alone, it looks far older than anything they've ever seen. Upon boarding, the scientists find the ship's occupants alive, but not exactly human.*

29. *An unnamed character loves relaxing in the field and eating grapes straight from the branch. While making another grab, the character hears a strange voice. The sound is garbled, but melodic and clear. They look down and find a tiny visitor from another world.*

30. *Most individuals assume aliens will utilize some sort of learnable language. But suppose the first contact doesn't include any form of verbal language. Instead, communication comes entirely from behavior.*

31.   *Late one night, an unnamed character is picking up their car from an impound lot. After providing the necessary paperwork, the character and attendant walk over to the car. They hear banging coming from inside the trunk. When they open it, they are startled to find a strange being inside.*

32.   *The first visitor is strong. Extremely so. No one quite knows where the alien came from, but most are too afraid to attempt opening dialogue with it. But there is one individual who thinks maybe—just maybe--they can communicate with it.*

33.   *Generally, everyone assumes humans will be the ones who will make first contact. But what if it isn't people at all? What if the first line of communication happens between aliens and one of Earth's other species?*

34.   *As many have predicted, first contact has had a great deal of negative undertones and aliens have come off as extremely aggressive. Their anger, however, has nothing to do with resources or the desire to take over humanity, but rather with the way they have been portrayed throughout history.*

35.   *A kid is obsessed with the concept of aliens. They spend most of their time in their bedroom reading books on the cosmos and whether it might hold other intelligent beings. Every night, this curious child sends out a message over a beat-up radio. One day they get a response.*

36. *Every year, the Perseid meteor shower occurs in the northern hemisphere during the months of August. While watching this wondrous display, an unnamed character sees a shower that doesn't quite look like any others. It gets closer and closer and then crashes some feet away. Against all rational, the character investigates the scene. They find a strange being that has been thrown from their spacecraft. Looking up, the alien begins to mutter in an unknown language.*

37. *If otherworldly beings do exist, what would their culture be like? Would they be religious in any way? Suppose these beings are religious and one tenant of their holy text is after they die, they will live in a paradise. Thus, after crash landing, an alien visitor mistakes Earth for their version of the afterlife. The other living beings, of course, are entirely unexpected.*

38. *First contact comes through a strange form of telepathy. At once, half of the world's population receives a message, right inside their mind. The other half can't figure out if they are lucky or unlucky for not receiving these odd alien messages.*

39. *Late one night, a group of teenagers go "ghost hunting" in a neighborhood cemetery. While making ghastly noises at each other and laughing loudly, one of them notices a shadow near one of the graves. It's not a ghost they find, but it is definitely something out of this world.*

40. *Deep within one of the hottest deserts on the planet, a group of scientists discover a collection of odd stones. After studying them, they figure out they are made from a composite not found on Earth. On a whim, one of the scientists begins arranging the stones in different patterns. One renders a giant wormhole and out steps an alien.*

41. *While outside playing an instrument, an unnamed character hears strange humming that echoes their exact melody. The musician plays a little faster and finally lures an alien out from where they have been hiding.*

42. *A group of teens decide to go skinny-dipping in a lake. There, they spot a horrific sight—a body! One of them wades out to it and screams. The body isn't human. Now the group must decide if they are going to alert the authorities or take care of the alien themselves.*

43. *An alien and a human meet for the first time in the history of their species. Each wants to ask the other so many questions, but there's a problem. They are both incredibly shy.*

44. *A group of aliens are ordered to observe the Earthlings and nothing more. One of them makes a bet with the others. The one that pranks the humans the best wins. At once, the group begins to outdo each other. It isn't before long first contact is inadvertently made.*

45. *While exploring deep within the cavernous area of a remote region, a group of archaeologists find a strange structure that looks man-made. But, it isn't man-made. In fact, it*

hasn't been touched by humans at all. Further still, the
creator of these strange artifacts is still lurking nearby.

Abduction

This would be a fourth level contact and the basis for many popular science fiction stories. It all began with Betty and Barney Hill who were allegedly abducted in 1961. Since then, alien abduction has been reported all over the world, with various degrees of evidence. No matter what you believe, the idea of humans being taken by otherworldly explorers against their will makes for a very compelling piece.

46. *An unnamed character has feelings they can't quite explain. Over and over, they are compelled to be at a certain spot, at a certain time. It's a force they cannot control, and time and time again, they find themselves planted at that very spot. That's when they show up.*

47. *While driving in a car over the freeway, an unnamed character suddenly loses control of the wheel. To make matters worse, the car pushes forward and drives over the railing. Before hitting the ground, the character is halted midair and vanishes from sight.*

48. *Curiously, an unnamed character is abducted straight out of their bedroom, bright beam of light and all. When they arrive aboard the mothership, they are placed at table with a strange being. On the table there are a bunch of strange metallic objects. In the center sits a realistic rendition of*

Earth. As it turns out, the character must play a game and if they lose, the planet no longer belongs to humans.

49. *The aliens are set in their religious beliefs. This includes ritualistic sacrifices as a means to appease their gods. Every 100 Earth years, a group of humans are taken for this purpose. On the 100th anniversary, this type of abduction includes a group of humans who refuse to go down without a fight.*

50. *On a faraway planet, these strange beings have a penchant for collecting species from other worlds. Sort of like humans owning pets. The more far flung the species comes from, the more valuable the "pet". One dealer hits a gold mine—a blue planet with billions of different Earthlings for the taking.*

51. *All world leaders have been abducted. The aliens take them hostage and make their demands. However, they did not bank on how uncooperative humans can be, especially if they have different political ideologies.*

52. *While running through the streets after a deal gone wrong, a streetwise con is abducted right where they stand. Once aboard the spaceship, the con immediately begins manipulating their way to freedom.*

53. *An abducted human finds a way to break out of their holding cell. They hope to find some kind of escape pod, but instead stumble across a chamber filled with frozen human bodies from many generations. At the last row, there is a*

vacant spot, one with the picture of the unnamed character right above it.

54. *Late one night, an unnamed character is woken by the sound of their small dog. Thinking the dog has to go outside, the character opens the door. As it swings wide, they vanish from sight. The only one left to tell the tale is the dog, who can only bark its shock.*

55. *Bleary eyed, a human wakes to find themselves on top of an examination table aboard an alien spacecraft. Horrified, they look around and see another table with strange and sharp tools. They can't be sure, but they have a sneaking suspicion that if they don't act fast, they'll be getting a closer look at them soon enough.*

56. *An abducted human is pondering their future inside a holding cell when they hear two aliens talking nearby. Although they do not understand the language, they understand pantomiming well enough. The aliens are deciding what to do with the human: throw them off the ship or destroy them where they stand.*

57. *For centuries, mankind has been abducted and used for experimentation. It usually ends badly for the abductees, but this time the group of humans have a plan and it involves using of their comrades as bait. The question is, which one?*

58. *An unnamed character has been abducted and returned safe from harm. At least, physically they are okay. Despite the very detailed and very convincing story, no one believes*

them. *Desperate to prove their strange tale, the character waits in the exact same spot they were taken every day, hoping this time they will get their proof.*

59. *In a small hamlet, long ago, children begin to go missing every full moon. The villagers are frightened and convinced it must be werewolves. Only one character knows the truth: the real culprits are beings that come from the sky.*

60. *Every night before bed, a child refuses to go to sleep. They claim if they close their eyes, the alien will come back. The child's parents are convinced it's just a stage, so to prove there is no otherworldly beings, they set up a video camera in the child's bedroom. The next day the family gathers together to have a look. Sure enough, the child vanishes out of bed only to be returned a few hours later.*

61. *One unnamed character has just had a horrific event. They have been abducted right from their bed. It's a traumatic event, made worse by the fact the character has just passed a significant birthday milestone (ex. 13th, 25th, etc.). The event is scary, but it's even scarier to talk to someone because they are certain they won't be believed. One day they cannot take the emotional toll and breakdown to a loved one. The loved one claims the exact same thing has happened to them. What's worse, it's happened for generations.*

62. *The first group of humans on Earth are also the first to have been abducted by aliens. What might happen to them as they are out amongst the stars? Furthermore, what might*

they be like when they come back and their primitive mind can't comprehend what has just happened?

63. *A filmmaker is doing a series documentary on alien abduction. After pouring through thousands of photographs and hundreds of tapes, and interviewing as many people as they can, they finally sense a pattern. Determined to make the piece as authentic as possible, they lure the aliens into abducting them, camera at the ready.*

64. *One Halloween night, a group of aliens have been tasked to abduct a bunch of humans to meet quota. Their forms are very close to some of the costumes that are being worn by the humans below. Unwittingly, one of the aliens accidentally abducts one of their own during the chaos.*

65. *One unnamed character is presented with a real "Sophie's Choice" type of scenario. The alien visitor only needs to abduct one human and the unnamed character must determine which loved one it will be.*

66. *Every couple of years, a group of humans are abducted and then returned without harm--other than emotional trauma. A paranormal investigator decides to study the phenomena and realizes these abductees aren't without physical trauma as they once thought. Instead, they have been micro chipped. It seems the aliens have been cataloging and studying humans for centuries.*

67. *Sleep paralysis is a real disorder in which an individual is unable to move during sleep and often claims to experience supernatural events. Although many debunk any kind of*

paranormal activity during one of these episodes, imagine if they were true. Sleep is the only way aliens can transport humans from one world to the next, even if the experience is entirely out-of-body.

68. *While most assume alien technology would cause an easier transport of humans—simply beam up and beam back down—this may not have always been the case. Envision earlier alien abductions when these otherworldly beings had not perfected the technique and an unnamed character suffers from it.*

69. *A line from a local advertising spot reads: "Have you been abducted and made to suffer at the hands of little green men? Do visitors from another world interrupt your precious sleep? Well, worry no more, friend. Simply call 1-800-Make-Em-Pay." An unnamed character decides to place a call.*

70. *Across the world humans are being abducted at a rapid pace. Meanwhile, across the universe, on an entirely different planet, the price of meat begins to go down.*

71. *While pouring through secret government documents, a paranormal investigator finds something unusual about an abduction case—a notation about receiving a specific organic material. Thinking it is a fluke, they find a similar notation in another abduction case. As it turns out, people weren't being abducted on a whim. They were being sold.*

72. *The government has finally disclosed the concept of alien abductions. While this normally would create a mini panic,*

in this case, it does not. Instead, the world accepts the fact they might be taken at any moment, and they ostracize those who have been abducted. What might the world be like if there is a new form of prejudice taking place?

73. *Supposedly, cows are one of the many animals that have been taken and tested on. In this scenario, imagine this is true, but instead of being mutilated or otherwise harmed, the cows come back able to understand any human language. And they sure do have a lot to say!*

74. *For experimentation purposes, two humans have been abducted and then placed in a cell together. Things are already strange for them because of the lack of clothes. But the situation gets even stranger when music begins to play and a human-type bed glides out of a wall. Turns out, this is a reproduction experiment.*

75. *An unnamed character continually visits a therapist over abduction claims. The therapist does not believe them, but the character represents a very easy payout because their tales are continuous. Then one night two alien visitors show up at the therapist's office and demand they destroy all "evidence".*

76. *After being presumably abducted, an unnamed character now finds themselves interrogated by government agents. The scene is so intense, the character can't quite decide which is worse: the abduction they have experienced, or the belief they have information the agents seek.*

77.	*While in the middle of taking a selfie, a teen suddenly vanishes without a trace. One of the onlookers picks up their phone and finds the teen was recently photobombed by an alien no one else saw.*

78.	*Desperate to get some new clients, an insurance agent begins to peddle alien insurance for when "they come for you". The agent thinks it's a load of bunk and only wants the sale. Until one day they are taken.*

79.	*At once, 10% of the world's population disappears. Although most of the world's religious leaders blame the phenomenon on some type of rapture, the reality is most definitely aliens.*

80.	*Consider the above scenario, but this time suppose those who have been abducted leave their bodies behind. It is like everyone is merely sleeping.*

81.	*Missing time is a common theme in most alien abductions. In this scenario, imagine if an abductee could suddenly account for everything that happened to them during that strange duration.*

82.	*Almost everyone in the world has been abducted at one point in their lives, even if they don't know it. The only telltale signs are implants hidden deep within the subject's brains. One day the implants suddenly start transmitting the exact same signal.*

83.	*An unnamed character receives coupons for an all expenses paid cruise. Upon arrival, the character finds out the ship doesn't exactly go into the sea. It flies through the air.*

84.   An unnamed character runs into the ER claiming they have been abducted by aliens and experimented on. While contacting the psychology department, the doctor on staff entertains the scared "victim" with a checkup, only to find they are missing a few organs.

85.   There are many products on the market designed to prevent alien abductions. This character has tried them all. What they don't account for is the fact aliens don't want anything to do with them. They want a loved one instead.

86.   An unnamed character has a horrible drug habit. During their infamous "episodes", they always have the same hallucination—they are visited and then taken by an otherworldly visitor. Eventually, the visitations seem so real, they decide to clean up their act. Later, they realize the incidents were real.

87.   An unnamed character receives a deal from a strange visitor they cannot pass up. All they have to do is abduct some unsuspecting victims and hand them over to the weird people in the flying saucer. Seems easy enough.

88.   A group of strangers awaken to find themselves trapped inside a giant maze. In the middle, is a portal that will send only one back home to Earth. Surrounding the maze, are thousands of cheering alien spectators.

89.   An alien abducts a human who begins to regale them about the alien movies, TV shows, comics, and other media they have seen. After four hours of nonstop talking, the alien decides to take the human back.

90.   *After a human is abducted, they are determined to make the most out of their horrible ordeal. As a result, they give interviews, start working on a documentary, and even launch a new merchandising line about the aliens that supposedly took them. One night, while they are casually sitting in their new penthouse, the aliens show back up and demand the human retract everything they've said...or else.*

Invasion

Famed theoretical physicist and cosmologist Stephen Hawking has an unfortunate theory about the potential of alien visitors. He believes if aliens do exist, then invasion would be the most likely scenario. To him, invasion would be imminent because traveling across the stars is so difficult. It has to have a purpose. So, logically, these little green men will come to Earth to utilize its resources and they will stop at nothing to get them. That's just theory, though. We don't *really* have anything to worry about, do we?

91.   *It has been 40 years since first contact was made. A neutral alliance is what they claimed would take place, and for those 40 years that's exactly what happened. However, it wasn't before long that one of ours killed one of theirs. Now the alliance is broken.*

92.   *Do aliens have a moral code? It's a question many wonder about. If they do, perhaps this moral code prevents them from killing living things? Still, these beings from another*

world want our resources. How might this problem be solved?

93. *The tide is turning in favor of the alien invaders. Humanity has been pushed deep into underground caves. The otherworldly beings are in the process of eradicating all human life. To complete that goal, they finally show up at the entry point.*

94. *Humans are being harvested for food by their alien overlords. While humans aren't the most ideal food option, the aliens believe they are special because of their immense intelligence. Proving that theory correct, the humans begin to plot various ways they can be a less ideal option.*

95. *The aliens that visit and invade are gigantic--at least 20 feet. The humans are easily at a disadvantage, but soon they discover the aliens' biggest weakness. They call it the "Achilles' Heel".*

96. *The aliens came for Earth's resources. A deal was reached that allowed a certain percentage to be used by aliens and the rest by humans. Before long, one side is found out to be undercutting the other.*

97. *Invasion has already occurred and it did not go in humanity's favor. The last of the human cities lay in ruins, and the aliens are enslaving the survivors. Little do they know, there is another human civilization amongst the cosmos, and their help is on the way.*

98. *The invaders expected the humans to be weak opponents. What they got instead was a technology far superior than*

their own. Other than interstellar travel and
communications, the humans excel at everything else.

99. *No matter how hard they try, the humans can't seem to get*
an upper advantage. Whatever move they make, the aliens
react instantly. That's when the human captain locates the
traitor.

100. *Social media is ablaze with reports of invading beings from*
another world. Many accounts are reporting a play-by-play
of what is going on. What the humans don't realize is that
this is exactly what the aliens want.

101. *They invaded humanity for their "own good", thinking they*
were an inferior species. They controlled everything, from
the new languages to the monetary system. In short, aliens
wanted to make humans exactly like them.

102. *The spaceships began to drop localized bombs that were*
meant to contain the damage so that natural resources
were preserved. That was their folly. They didn't count on
humans sacrificing many nations to save their own.

103. *The invasion happened out of the blue. One minute the*
humans were going about their daily life, and the next a
torrent of spacecrafts were reigning down. After the dust
settled and most of humanity was lost, the aliens realized
one important fact – they had the wrong planet.

104. *Humanity is so addicted to technology, it would not be*
surprising if that's how the tide of war swung in the aliens'
favor. Imagine how this wave of technology destruction
might occur in an alien invasion. No communication,

damages to homes and infrastructure, etc. Now imagine
what humanity would do to turn all of that around and
win.

105. *These aliens are smart and their weapon is on the*
microscopic level. They invent a pathogen that would work
to wipe out the dominate species--humans. It starts with a
cough and by the time the billionth individual in infected,
that is when they start to arrive.

106. *By now, the humans and aliens are involved in guerrilla*
warfare and it is not looking for good the earthlings. Most
live in underground tunnels and attack using makeshift
weapons since manufacturing has been halted. One brave
character discovers a section of the tunnel exists right over
an alien encampment, giving them access to a full arsenal
of alien weaponry.

107. *To give themselves a better advantage, humans rely on a*
Greek military tactic—The Trojan Horse. Only this time,
the "horse" is a collection of humans meant to be a type of
sacrificial peace offering under the slogan "spare few, save
many". What the aliens didn't account for was the humans
sent over are some of the strongest, bravest, and best
fighters in the world.

108. *Knowing their own world is dying, the humans have*
studied the alien planet for the past hundred years. They
are a peaceful loving society, with a technology far superior.
Many religious groups commend the attacks, but at the

same time everyone agrees: something must be done before Earth is no longer inhabitable.

109. A military attack on one of the most influential nations has occurred. Surprisingly, it has been linked to an ally. Before long, another World War breaks out. With advanced technologies, many fear these aggressions will foster the end of humanity. Meanwhile, the aliens sit back and wait.

110. Alien infiltration is a common theme in science fiction and is quite different than assimilation. In assimilation, the goal is peaceful cohabitation, while in infiltration the goal is to completely overtake the human species. Such is the case in this scenario, where alien invaders are nothing more than pathogenic organisms that are slowly taking over the bodies of humanity.

111. Suppose the above scenario holds true and there are small, intelligent organisms that are able to take over human bodies to do their bidding. In this scenario, consider these organisms do not attack all humans, but instead latch onto one that holds a significant amount of influence.

112. Invaders have infiltrated humans not by organisms, but by their advanced cloaking technology. To learn more about their enemies they have begun the first wave of invasion: owning homes, living, and working amongst the humans. One keen individual swears their neighbour is one, but there's a problem – nobody believes them!

113. Another popular idea of science fiction stories involving invasion is the idea of terraforming. This occurs when the

35

earth is shaped in order to be conducive to live. In this case, it's alien life. The aliens are a farming race that do not care about humans at all, as long as they stay out of the way while the earth is completely transformed. This transformation makes it more liveable for the alien and their needs, but not so much for the humans.

114. After humanity is on the brink of destruction--mostly because of their own poor choices--an alien race begins to send over "care packages". This is loaded with food that is suppose to offset the current food shortage. Only the humans don't know the food isn't food at all, but poison meant to finish the job.

115. The humans have given the aliens a set contract: mine the planet for a certain amount of years in exchange for weaponry and then move on. The weaponry is supposed to be used against the enemies of the humans who made the deal. But it isn't long before this technology is used against the aliens themselves.

116. Suppose the above scenario holds true, but there is no contract in place. Instead, the aliens have taken over Earth and only plan to stay on the planet until all resources have been completely stripped away. This means the aliens will move on after a certain period of time, which means the humans will survive. It also means the humans will no longer have natural resources and will die a slow death.

117. After a war has raged on for several years, the alien side finally has an upper advantage – they have stolen the child

of one of the biggest leaders on Earth. Now negotiations begin. Mix up this scenario and have the humans steal an alien child from the invading army.

118. Invasion comes in small raids. First, rural farms are hit all over the world by mysterious "night bandits". When these results prove successful, suburban communities are hit. By the time the aliens begin to raid cities, the humans figure out it isn't criminals from their own species. It is something out of this world.

119. Earth has been declared a natural reservation by an alien race. They want to preserve the sanctity of the planet to conserve its beauty. That's why they must control the parasite that is destroying Mother Nature from the inside out – the humans.

120. The aliens have long observed how the humans treat each other, ending the lives of innocents and destroying whole countries. After another war breaks out, the aliens finally decide to invade. They need to teach the humans a better way to live. But first, the human race must be conquered and then made to listen.

121. Imagine alien invaders have once visited the earth in the past (the historic time is entirely up to you). In this scenario, no matter what time period it is, the aliens have caused it to happen to set humanity on a specific course that is now coming to a head.

122. "War of the Worlds" by Orson Welles is one of the most infamous alien invasion stories on the planet. It even

caused a stir when it was read live over the radio. In this scenario, imagine the aliens used this fabricated event to attack, knowing the fake story would be a good cover for the actual invasion.

123. *Aliens have become a significant ally for the human resource, offering new foods, technology, medicine, and even new methods of culture. This was all intended as a subversive plan to gain the humans' trust. Once they have it, the aliens attack.*

124. *Humans are at war with aliens and things are getting bleak. That's when another otherworldly species shows up, helping humanity fight off these foreign invaders. With their new alien allies, the battle shifts in the other direction.*

125. *These alien invaders are rather crafty and spend years cultivating the perfect plan. No one notices when birth rates begin to drop, blaming it on lack of food resources, overpopulation, and other such factors. But when they stop completely, that's when the aliens make their appearance.*

126. *Aliens use mind-numbing reality television against us. No one realizes the alien owned network is just that – owned by aliens. But they do catch wind of all of the new shows. Reality content they won't get on any other channel. What they don't know is it begins to slowly rot their brains, so when the aliens attack, the humans don't care.*

127. *The aliens didn't mean to invade our planet, not really. It started with an accidental space crash—not exactly a world*

ending scenario. The only problem? The alien spaceship was the size of a small city.

128.   *Piggybacking on the idea aliens might not mean to outright destroy Earth, suppose the aliens that come are refuges. Perhaps their own home planet has even been invaded. In this scenario, the aliens happen to produce young at a rapid pace, and before long many generations of this alien species is destroying the resources meant for humans.*

129.   *The alien invaders are strong, and fighting them is proving to be problematic. It is like all of these otherworldly beings are one unit, outsmarting their opponents at every turn. One brave human soldier discovers why the aliens seem so uniform: they are being controlled by a hive mind. If the humans can find and locate this "brain", then they might have a chance to survive.*

130.   *In any proper invasion you have to have a little leverage, right? The aliens have studied humans enough to know they could easily get over their comrades being taken. But their pets? That's a different story.*

Assimilation

Going back to Hynek's six classification theory, we will now be dealing with contact 5 - 7. At this stage, there is a lot of potential for a good story. Assimilation is a varied term and encompasses the idea of aliens peacefully becoming a part of daily Earth life, or living amongst humans without their knowledge.

131. *A woman comes into the emergency room complaining of extreme abdominal pain. After a multi-test evaluation, doctors claim there is nothing physically wrong with her. That is, until she goes into labor.*

132. *A child is born who speaks by the end of the first year, reads and writes by the second, and masters physics by the third. Everyone is amazed by this child prodigy, saying they will surely become the smartest person to have ever lived. There's just one problem: this child isn't completely human.*

133. *While working in an ER, a doctor gets a patient who is acting very odd. They are going through the usual methods of checkup when suddenly the patient doubles over in pain. Then, bit by bit, their flesh flecks off, revealing the hidden alien body beneath.*

134. *Police have been investigating rival gangs for quite some time now to get a jump on the drugs that have plagued the city. In the dead of night, a hapless rookie is staking out a known hideout when he sees something that rocks him to his core: one by one the group of gang members remove their skin before entering the building. Curiously, they all take a whiff of the "drugs" beforehand.*

135. *Though assimilation typically deals with aliens living amongst humans, let's say the reverse is true. Against their best judgment, a being from another world, who looks very similar to us, abducts an infant. No matter if it was infatuation with the human race or mere curiosity, the*

infant is now approaching the teenage years and other members of the alien species are starting to get suspicious.

136. *On the eve of their wedding, two newlyweds sit down to discuss their future together. The conversation goes into normal territory: future house, kids, pets. Then it goes in a new and strange direction. One fiancée reveals to the other they haven't been entirely truthful. No, it's not a secret lover. It's the fact they aren't human.*

137. *There are governmental labs placed all over the world, and many deal with infectious diseases. While the assumption is these diseases are manmade and are created as part of biological warfare experiments, perhaps they are actually alien-made. In this scenario, picture a world in which aliens live and work amongst these labs, hidden in secret away from public eye.*

138. *The aliens have advanced technology that allows them to cloak their forms to the naked eye. Thus, when the idea of "shadow people" is put forth by one scientist, no one believes their theories. That is, until they invent a device (be it pill, eyewear, etc.) that allows others to see these invisible aliens.*

139. *The aliens have assimilated well with Earth's environment, taking on the form of trees, flowers, and other types of plants. Thus, when humans begin to tear up the ecosystem, it isn't long before a hapless worker discovers their secret.*

140. *Parasitic aliens find humans are not viable hosts as their immune systems are too far advanced, likely aided by*

medicine. Instead, the aliens begin to inhabit the bodies of animals, especially those closest to humans. As a result, a plethora of mutant species are starting to develop.

141. *The aliens may be a peaceful race, but they are also an extremely religious one. So far, they have managed to convert 1/10th of the population, and it isn't long before they come knocking at a character's door who can either listen or fight the proposed indoctrination.*

142. *Aliens and humans now live in peaceful cohabitation. Well, almost peaceful. The aliens are a benevolent race that are extremely useful because they enjoy the sunshine and tilling the land, never consuming more than their fair share. The problem is they insist on using great big beasts, brought from their planet, to fertilize the soil. These beasts become problematic and the humans must decide if their new alien cohorts are worth all of this trouble.*

143. *When the aliens came down, humans were completely enraptured by them. Some were in awe of their advanced technology, others of their ability to communicate with humans. However, a small collection of humans were interested in…other ways. In fact, a whole subculture began to center around alien fetishists who called themselves "starmappers".*

144. *Consider the above scenario. But rather than giving you free reign of what might happen with that concept, picture what might happen if a club formed around this strange fetish. Now imagine what might happen if it was suddenly*

invaded by police; not because of the culture itself, but because of something else entirely.

145. *The aliens came with their advanced technology, but also with their diseases. At first, it was a small coughing disease, akin to the common cold. But, as it turns out, this disease evolves at a rapid pace, and several mutations later, it's unstoppable.*

146. *They have been here for thousands of years, forming their own societies and becoming more advanced as time went on. In fact, in many ways, the rise of their evolution coincided greatly with our own. Why haven't we noticed them before? Because they live in the deepest part of the oceans, often known as the Challenger Deep. It isn't until a lonely expedition when an underwater explorer sees one for the first time from their small one-person sub.*

147. *Consider the above scenario, except these aliens do not live in the deepest of waters. They have chosen a location near a port where it's shallower to take advantage of the copious amount of sea life for food. While swimming in the waters one day, a small child spots what they think is a mermaid.*

148. *The aliens that live amongst us have become addicted to cattle after trying a juicy steak--done rare. The humans only meant to introduce them to the gluttonous meal. They didn't realize the aliens would become so entranced by the feast they would go out of their way to hunt the hapless bovine.*

149. *The lifespan of an alien models a human's closely. As a result, poor decision making is often seen during the teenage years. The teen aliens have been warned by their parents not to try alcoholic substances because if lab results are any indication, it will not do well with their species. After a dare from their human friends, these teen aliens think one drink won't hurt.*

150. *Humans and aliens get along well. They live in the same neighborhoods, work at the same jobs, and have a peaceful coexistence. Little do they know there's a secret government facility where aliens are being experimented on. One day, a hapless alien stumbles upon these horrific facts.*

151. *The majority of humanity does not know of the existence of aliens, despite the fact the government allows them to live and work amongst them. Although the government gives them—more or less—free reign to do what they please, they have created a classification system to keep track of the many alien species living on planet Earth. For this scenario, create this classification system, including what types of aliens might be classified.*

152. *The "Adopt Alien Pets" campaign is in full swing when it is discovered another planet hosts life, though not very intelligent life. The species that inhabit this planet are of the cute and small variety, with the best part being they do not make a great deal of messes and require very little food. Due to their easy maintenance, many people clamor to*

purchase some of these new species. What could possibly go wrong?

153. *A few years ago, former Canadian Defense Minister Paul Hellyer claimed there are approximately 80 different species of aliens living on our planet for "thousands of years". Why haven't we noticed these aliens before? Hellyer claims it's because these aliens are completely turned off by the way we handle our planet, especially with the overwhelming pollution that takes place. Suppose this scenario is true, and further, suppose these aliens have finally had enough.*

154. *Imagine the Salem Witch trials involved persons accused of witchcraft, but rather than being mere innocent persons or actual witches, these poor souls were actually aliens sent here long ago to study our kind.*

155. *In the concept of the Prime Directive, which is created from "Star Trek", certain planetary regulations prohibit one from interfering with alien civilizations through advancement. Essentially, no technology, values, culture, etc. should be placed on the alien race for the purpose of evolution or indoctrination. Suppose there is a "mad scientist" type of alien that wants to know what will happen if they assimilate with the humans to teach them.*

156. *Consider a similar scenario in which aliens are sent to Earth for observational purposes only. They are meant only to record interactions on a personal level to gather more scientific data for their research. This means they cannot*

directly interfere in the lives of humans. So far, the aliens have not been spotted and everything is going fine. Then an alien witnesses a human they have grown fond of being attacked and the only way to save them is to reveal themselves.

157. *While hiking through the woods one day, a human couple runs across a log cabin that has purple smoke coming from it. No one has really ventured this far off trail before, but the couple got lost after a fight (or perhaps another reason). They decide to approach the cabin to get directions. There, they find a small collection of aliens that have been living in the area for several years.*

158. *A group of children are playing outside when one of them spots a glinting object in the distance. Thinking it might be a toy or, better yet, an adult object they aren't supposed to touch, they make a grab for it. As it turns out, the object is alien in nature and the owner isn't too far behind.*

159. *If there is one thing that remains true throughout history it is that humans generally rebel against things that are different than them. Chances are, if aliens were found to be living amongst us, protests would be imminent. Some sides would be rallying around the aliens, believing they should be allowed to live as humans do. Others would be demanding they be sent back to wherever they came, or worse, that they should be executed. Others are seeking the ability to allow experimentation. Create a narrative in*

which all of these groups exist, and then determine whose voice will ultimately be the loudest.

160. *Imagine aliens have visited Earth in the past and, due to their primitive nature and lack of intelligence, the humans regard them as some type of divine being. For this prompt, consider two scenarios: Pen a tale that takes place during this time, or envision what history might be like if this change were to take place.*

161. *A group of aliens have been living peacefully among the human populace. One day they are found out by a cruel hunter who vows they will be hunted down. The aliens must choose between breaking their own rule of peace or protecting themselves from potential annihilation.*

162. *Aliens have been living amongst the human population for centuries. The humans aren't aware of it because the aliens can easily camouflage themselves in the foliage. But with environmental damage destroying much of their habitat, the aliens decide it's time to come out of hiding and say something.*

163. *An alien scout has lived with the human for a few years now, pretending to be a human child. They've even gone as far as being placed with a human family through a fake adoption. Generally, they use a type of mimicry to sound exactly like the humans. Little did they know that too much soda would have a drastic effect on their alien vocal cords. It isn't long before they are found out.*

164. *A new motivational speaker is taking the world by storm. Using their "Path to the Stars" mindset, this speaker encourages everyone to find a certain path that will lead them to success. Some might say this speaker's tactics are a little out of this world.*

165. *The grand opening of a new restaurant is receiving rave reviews. The atmosphere and aesthetics is great, but people really come here for the food. What patrons don't know is the restaurant owners just happen to be aliens and the food isn't exactly local.*

166. *An alien couple has been living on Earth for quite some time now. When they near the end of their natural lifecycle they send a message back home about how much they've enjoyed their time on this strange blue planet. It isn't long before other elderly aliens begin to migrate to the planet, making Earth their unofficial retirement home.*

167. *A member of an elite alien scouting crew has been sent to Earth to assimilate in order to learn more about the humans. Despite the fact this alien is known for being stoic, it isn't long before they become obsessed with human vices—from drinking to picking up strangers at bars.*

168. *At a board meeting for one of the top billion dollar corporations in the country, a CEO is giving a riveting motivational speech about the next quarter. They take a break to go to the bathroom. That's when an unnamed character spots them doing something that isn't exactly human.*

169. *Bigfoot, Lochness, and other mythical creatures are often cited as being from remote parts of Earth. The fact they originated from this planet is easily understood, but what if that were not the case? Craft a narrative in which one of these mythical creatures actually have alien origins and that is why they have rarely been spotted.*

170. *An alien lands on Earth expecting to assimilate among humans and learn more about the culture. For a few days, this plan goes without a hitch. Then the alien realizes they are not susceptible to diseases in the environment, something they have never experienced before.*

171. *Seeing what humans have done with the planet, a small group of aliens begin to conspire with some Earth animals to overthrow the parasites.*

172. *While at a concert, an unnamed character notices a member of the crowd does not look like anyone else. Even though it's the middle of summer, they are wearing warm clothes and are fully covered up. After following them, the character is convinced it's an alien. Now they just have to find proof.*

173. *While exploring the basement of their new home, a lonely child discovers an alien who has been living there for a long time. Rather than tell their parents, the child befriends the alien and quickly learns to use telepathy to talk to it.*

174. *An Earth family takes in a wayward alien orphan as part of a secret governmental program. They aren't supposed to tell anyone and are ordered to raise the alien as one of their*

own. What the government doesn't tell them, however, is that this alien race has a very unusual puberty stage.

175. *Imagine the above scenario holds true and the alien is actually being groomed to become an ambassador for their home planet. That is, if they can stop being transfixed by the television for two minutes. For a variation, the alien can be taken with the internet, video games, or any other mind-numbing Earth technology.*

176. *At an annual science fiction meeting the President finally makes an important announcement. A real live alien has not only been discovered, but they have been in their midst for the past few years. A member in the crowd is instantly angered. Their identity has just been revealed.*

177. *At a fancy dinner party, friends of the hosts uncover a strange fact: the mistress of the house is actually an alien. Of course, they come to this conclusion by almost destroying her home in the process. She is not mad at being revealed so much as she upset that her perfect casserole has been ruined.*

178. *The body count keeps rising in a small little community and very soon everyone is pointing fingers at each other. What they don't realize is the real culprit is the person you'd least expect it. Not only that, but the murderer is also secretly an alien.*

Alien Worlds

Who says we need to stay in Earth to pen a good alien tale? It is estimated there are approximately 5×10^{22} planets in the known universe alone. That's 50,000,000,000,000,000,000,000. With that number, there is a huge expansive potential for different cultures to spring up out of the cosmos.

179.   *The Earth is composed of approximately 96.5% water. However, what if this was not the case for this planet? What if the reverse was true and the creatures that inhabited it were made predominately of a rocky substance. Perhaps the change is slight, or perhaps this change leads to a great deal of significance in how these beings live their lives.*

180.   *Space explorers come to an alien planet that appears desolate and free of life. That is, until the explorers begin to descend below the surface of the planet and find a whole alien civilization living underneath the rocky terrain.*

181.   *After crash landing on an alien environment, a human crew is taken hostage by the aliens that inhabit the planet. The aliens are amused by these strange beings, and show their amusement by bestowing a great honor upon them— allowing them to fight to the death in a type of Roman Coliseum.*

182.   *Survivors of a rocket crash find themselves in an environment similar to Earth. The only problem is the similarity is about a million years different than the time the humans hail from.*

183.   *A spaceship explodes. Thankfully, a group of survivors manage to get out in time via escape pods. The only problem is they are all headed to entirely different planets.*

184.   In a scenario akin to "Jack and the Beanstalk", explorers to
        an alien planet find a race of large giants that are very
        similar to humans in their appearance. In fact, the culture
        also bears a striking resemblance, complete with these
        beings' penchant for hoarding gold and other precious
        minerals that would be highly valuable back home on
        Earth.

185.   Explorers visit a planet that's alien culture is primitive in
        its ways. When these strange earthlings are viewed, it isn't
        with disdain or horror, but instead divine worship.

186.   Consider the above scenario, but instead of all the group
        being worshiped and revered, what if only one from the
        group fulfils some type of perceived alien prophecy. It does
        not matter the reason. What really matters is one, or all, of
        the others in the group are insanely jealous.

187.   Humans must find a way to terraform a newly discovered
        planet to ensure survival of the human race. Only there's a
        problem – this planet is already occupied.

188.   An alien planet is discovered to have resources that are
        1,000 times superior than the best energy source on Earth.
        Even just taking a small fraction of these strange minerals
        will power every home in the planet for the next century or
        so. The humans desperately want to take it back to their
        planet, but first, they must bypass the strange and vicious
        alien creatures that live on this new world.

189.   Consider the above scenario, but rather than there being
        primitive alien creatures that are mere predators, instead

there are intelligent beings that inhabit this resource-rich planet. In this scenario, either negotiation or outright military attack would be the only outcome in bringing these minerals back to Earth.

190. While exploring a strange planet that is only compromised of docile creatures, one human becomes attached to one of the more "adorable" aliens. Although they are not supposed to take anything back, as this is a expeditionary mission, the astronaut still attempts to smuggle their new friend into the spaceship.

191. One of the more popular alien world science fiction tropes is the idea the aliens might be giant bug-like monsters. In this scenario try to picture what that might be like and build your narrative around a spacecraft that has crash landed on this strange planet.

192. On the opposite end of the spectrum, for the above scenario envision this planet is composed of bug like aliens that are not giant, but very small. These aliens are not unlike bugs seen on Earth, only on this planet, they are highly evolved, intelligent, and consider the exploring humans a threat.

193. In a exploratory mission, astronauts come across an alien race that invites them into their midst. Although the language is known by the humans, they try their best to interact with the aliens, unaware they are actually negotiating the sale of Earth.

194. When a spacecraft lands on an alien planet, the survivors count themselves lucky. There is enough food and water on

board to ensure survival while the spaceship is being fixed. If worse comes to worst, the humans have also located some resources on the planet themselves. What they aren't aware of, however, is there is a species on the planet that is not only intelligent, but is willing to feed on any kind of meat that happens their way – even one as advanced as they are.

195. *While working outside the spaceship, an astronaut's tether becomes loose and they are thrown into the gravitational pull of a nearby planet. The suits are advanced enough to survive the fall, but the planet itself is filled with a great deal of danger – from the aliens that inhabit the planet to the volatile ecosystem. The stranded astronaut must figure out a way to survive while those back on board the spaceship must consider if they are worth saving.*

196. *Humans have finally managed to reach a point where they no longer pollute the planet and have found a new way of sustainable living. This has advanced the world's newly created collective space program several hundred years. This is also why when another planet is discovered with aliens that seem to be headed down the same path of self-destruction humans were once on, the astronauts are eager to offer some advice.*

197. *After finding a planet that is rich with natural resources, a group of astronauts make a pact to mine the planet and split all of their earnings. The more they begin to mine the planet, the more each of them begin to wonder if splitting*

*the profits are more ideal than simply doing away with the
others.*

198. *A team of scientists visit an alien planet to study the
unintelligent life that lives there. As it turns out, these
aliens are not so dumb after all. In fact, they are more
advanced than originally thought and it is they who want
to gather up these humans for study, especially through an
"alien" autopsy.*

199. *When humans crash land on this alien planet, they are
given food, water, and shelter. Since this planet is so similar
to Earth and the aliens' biology is equally put together, both
the aliens and humans assume all is well. That is, until the
first survivor becomes ill.*

200. *They call this planet "New Earth" and it is meant to replace
the planet that will not last much longer. Back home, a
movement develops between those that believe the current
Earth can be saved and refuse to let it go, versus those who
believe this new planet is the only option. To force the hand
of these naysayers, those who dub themselves "true
earthlings" begin to devise a way to destroy New Earth.*

201. *After exploring an alien planet, and being treated quite
well by this world inhabitants, the explorers are now ready
to head back home. However, it seems the aliens' leader has
become infatuated with one of the survivors and will only
let the others go if this human stays behind forever.*

202. *Many individuals assume an alien world will be comprised
of only one type of intelligent species. After all, in Earth*

there is the humans and all of the other animals. In this scenario picture a planet where there are more than one species of intelligent beings, and when the humans land on this planet, they land in the middle of a war between them.

203. *After crash landing on an alien planet, the sole astronaut aboard knows they need to step out of the ship and either find some natural resources on the planet to restore the ship, or restore the ship by some other means. Stepping out proves to be a frightening option. They fear the shadowy figures hanging outside the ship, peering into the windows at every opportunity.*

204. *The humans thought they hit the jackpot when they discovered a planet that has an array of natural resources fit for humans – from edible plants that grow in the environment to previous minerals that can be mined. Although the humans knew nights lasted for 18 hours of one 24 cycle Earth day on this planet, what they didn't know was that strange alien creatures also came out during this time.*

205. *After Earth has been destroyed a group of survivors head out amongst the stars in hopes there is a planet viable enough to support human life. After thousands of years aboard the ship, a planet is finally found. But when they land there are already humanoid creatures that occupy this new planet. As it turns out, an exploratory mission was sent long ago, but the group of humans never made it back. They were alive, living on this planet. After years of*

removal from Earth society, these so-called humans are more alien to the survivors than anything else.

206.   An alien planet is found by stranded astronauts to contain a race that seems friendly enough and treats the humans well. In fact, since there is no way to get back home to Earth, these aliens suggest the humans stay and live on this new planet. This does not come without a cost. To live in this world, the demand is undergo cosmetic surgery in order to appear just like the aliens and better assimilate.

207.   A conference is held on a distant planet involving species from all across the galaxies. The subject up for discussion? Earth. The aliens want to decide whether or not to remove humans from the planet to ensure the survival of the other species that live there.

208.   In a tale befitting Romeo and Juliet, a human and an alien from another planet fall madly in love. The problem? The two species are bitter rivals so they must convince their kind not to destroy the other.

209.   An astronaut stumbles across a planet that not only holds life, but also a well defined culture. In a show of goodwill, the ambassadors to their planet invites the human to the queen's coronation ceremony. The species is so close to Earthlings the astronaut can't help but fall in love.

210.   A new planet is discovered with aliens of different species. Not only are they unintelligent, but there is talk they might be able to become a new food resource. Instantly, Earth is divided on what do with these potentially tasty creatures.

211. *After a lengthy time of searching and searching, humanity finally has proof there is life on another planet. Rather than wait for the aliens to come to Earth, a group of astronauts set out to visit the alien world, not knowing what they might find there.*

212. *An unnamed character is taken by surprise when their best friend turns out to be an alien. More surprisingly, the alien is homesick and wants to return to their planet. But they don't want to go alone.*

213. *An unnamed astronaut becomes stranded on a strange alien world. What makes this planet so strange isn't its inhabitants, but the lack of them despite the rich plant life that exists.*

214. *A spaceship crashes on a strange alien planet. If this was not bad enough it is soon realized this crash is part of a larger ruse. For several years now, aliens have been crashing Earth ships in order to conduct a planet wide "human hunts" for sport.*

215. *A human lands on an alien planet and is taken aback to find they look very similar to these strange beings. Of course, not entirely similar. Although the difference is obvious, many of these aliens downright refuse to believe this person is from somewhere called "Earth".*

Apocalypse, New Societies, & Cataclysmic Disasters.

The idea that society will change is one we cannot help but be fascinated by. What will the future hold? Usually the question is guided by an answer based off an entirely different social or political order. Typically, science fiction deals with future society in one of four ways:

- o **Post-Apocalyptic:** This subgenre of science fiction generally deals with the collapse of society. It can be through disease, overpopulation, outright war, or some other horrible atrocity.
- o **Dystopian:** Often confused with the post-apocalyptic genre, a dystopian deals with a society that gives up something in order to maintain total control. Oftentimes, this is at the expense of free will or the use of technology.
- o **Utopian:** What makes a perfect society? This subgenre seeks to answer it. A utopian is the idealized world where mankind has finally reached a state of perfection, whether that is in terms of technology, resources, social interaction, or a mix of everything.
- o **Post-Scarcity**[*]: This concept strictly deals with economics, or rather, it is projection of what life would be like if there were an infinite number of resources. We know scarcity creates problems for mankind, but what about the reverse end of the spectrum?

*Typically, post-scarcity is placed in either a dystopian or utopian narrative.

Now that you know the ins and outs of the differences in genre forms, let's go ahead and try to destroy the world as we know it.

Environment

Environmental problems are nothing new, and many are aware of the dangers of global warming, overpopulation, and so on. When dealing with a science fiction environmental disaster, the first thing is to consider how violently Mother Nature may revolt against her injuries and what mankind can do as a result.

216.   *Recently, a great deal of concern has been crafted around the potential environmental threat that comes with traditional Western burial practices. Many chemicals do not break down and can create toxicity within the environment. One solution is to breed certain types of mushrooms in such a way, they will begin to decay deceased human tissue. However, what if the reverse started to happen? What if these fungus types began to feed off of live tissue?*

217.   *An environmental disaster has occurred and an unnamed character is ill-prepared. They have to get to a safer environment, but do not have a "bug out" bag prepared for the long journey. Time is running out. They must act fast and grab as few items as possible to make the perilous trip*

before it's too late. Frame your narrative around these items and how they will be helpful en route to the safe destination.

218. *An unnamed character has been wandering for days after a cataclysmic disaster. They are thirst and hungry. If they do not satiate one of those problems, they know they will not last much longer. While wandering, they come across a large bog filled with strange looking fruit. They could easily eat the fruit, but it might be possible to use it as bait for some wayward animal.*

219. *A solar flare has completely caused many of the nations' electrical grid to fail. Not only are communications down, but many other effects are tearing apart the very fabric of modern society. Crews are working around the clock, but little do they know more solar flares are on the way.*

220. *A massive earthquake occurs in the northern hemisphere, causing collapsed buildings and extreme turmoil. A city on the edge of the coast has no idea the earthquake has happened. As a result, they are unaware of the large-scale tsunami coming.*

221. *One of the biggest theories surrounding the fall of the dinosaurs is an asteroid impact that caused cataclysmic results. Predictions constantly point out another one is inevitable. Toying with this idea, imagine a large meteor has just hit, completely destroying a major city filled with millions, if not billions of people. Now imagine some of the aftereffects: fires, tidal waves, and enough kicked up debris*

to block out the sun. The humans must now cope with the world where night seems eternal, and both plant and animal species are dying at a rapid pace.

222. Craft a story from the perspective of an ancient civilization who has just witnessed a volcano erupt for the first time. Imagine the awe and horror. More importantly, consider how they might work to survive in such a limited space. That is, if they survive at all.

223. To gauge risk, philosopher Nick Bostrom has created a classification system based on perceived risk and how it effects humanity. "Bangs" are catastrophes that occur suddenly, whether created or accidental. "Crunches" are when humanity survives, but the world will never be the same. "Shrieks" are an undesirable future for humankind. "Whimpers" are when human civilization, or some aspect of it, declines. Using an environmental disaster, utilize one of these risk factors to craft a narrative, paying close attention to how humans might react.

224. Humanity has finally reached a point where only 5% of all water on earth is safe to drink. Those who have are not willing to share. Those who do not have it are trying to desperately garner this precious, life sustaining resource— by force or through a new invention.

225. Honey bees and similar pollinators allow plants to distribute their genetic material, furthering the plant line. In a world without these important species, there are few vegetables, fruits, or any plant life. To survive in this new

world, humans have not only evolved to breath less oxygen, but they have also become almost 100% carnivores, even if that means they must eat opposing fractions of their own kind for nourishment.

226. *In another bee-related scenario, an unnamed character stumbles across a bee nest that turns out to be comprised of Africanized, or "killer bees". After subsequently being attacked, scientists are alerted these bees are an entirely new species. They still have the same aggressive nature, but they are much larger and their intelligence is on par with some species of birds. They are even able to recognize human faces and determine when they might pose a threat.*

227. *Climate change has created a huge dichotomy in the world as it takes up most of Earth's natural resources. There are the areas that have natural resources, and there are the areas that are devoid of life (be it a snowy tundra or bleak dessert). In this new world, there are two fractions to go along with these new environments, as the population requires dispersal. One group is known as "bone hunters" for their need to hunt wayward prey that ventures into the lands. The other side is known as "grass eaters" for their need to live off the natural resources of the land.*

228. *Ethologist, John B. Calhoun, is notable for his research into overpopulation using rodents. After increasing the rodent population in a controlled environment, he eventually saw the complete breakdown of social society. The conclusion: this may be man's future due to overpopulation. Notably,*

some members of the group were dubbed "the beautiful ones" because they completely detached from society and had no scars that usually cover males fighting for their territory. In essence, these rats only existed, not truly lived. Imagine this is man's fate, and craft a society where humans no longer interact with each other, reproduction has all but stopped, and it's likely humanity may not continue.

229. "Doomsday preppers" is the typical name given to those who are already planning for some potential cataclysmic event that creates an outright apocalypse. An unnamed character has been a doomsday prepper for most of their life and when the "big one" finally happens, they are ready. The environment is revolting, but they know exactly which safe zones to go to avoid most of the disasters. Do they start on the journey solo? Or do they go ahead and take their neighbours, despite being called nuts by them for years?

230. A worldwide drought has occurred, causing a surge in water prices and a clamor to take as many bottles off the shelf as possible. Luckily for one unnamed character, they have their own private lake which many do not know about due to its secluded nature. Unfortunately, it's just been spotted.

231. Massive hurricanes have almost eradicated the coastline of a major country. Homes lay in ruins and there is so much debris, it looks like the inside of a war zone. Despite that, a

group of characters must survive in the ruins despite the continued rain and the overall lack of resources.

232. *The Great Pacific Garbage patch is a huge collection of trash, sludge, and other debris left floating in the water. For obvious reasons, cleanup has been difficult and it has caused mayhem on the ecosystem. Imagine this patch has continued to grow to the point there is essentially no more ocean left and it has been replaced by this giant trash sludge. Now there's a vast reduction of fish, very little water, and a need to trudge through the trash to import and export goods.*

233. *Invasive species are organisms that are brought into a territory they are not native to. Generally, this can bring about negative consequences. In this scenario, an invasive species has been smuggled into an airport. Although the organism is only meant to be released upon landing, it escapes and the high altitude changes its body chemistry, creating dire consequences.*

234. *Bombs have been placed on approximately 120 ships and trains containing crude oil. They explode at once, creating major disasters in multiple parts of the world. Not only does this significantly impact transportation and energy, but the environmental effects could be cataclysmic.*

235. *To create a pesticide that is eco-friendly, a botanist has been toying with the idea of creating predatory plant species that is more effective at catching all kinds of threats to crops and small mammals. Over multiple generations,*

the botanist has finally evolved a plant not only large enough to eat this larger prey, but also mobile enough to seek it out. Only one problem. The latest generation has a taste for human flesh.

236. *Due to lack of dispersal room, trash slums have begun to appear all over the world. These citywide areas expand to the point whole societies are created. Since there is little room and little resources, those within this group begin to raid nearby "clean zones".*

237. *After multi-disasters strike Earth, it is a scramble to get to safety. There are those who are too weak or injured to make it out and will ultimately die, and there are those who are desperate to survive and will do whatever it takes. And then there are the "units", groups of people who have banded together because of their survival skills. Recently, units have begun transferring people out of the danger zones, often trekking across hazardous areas. The problem is, not everyone can afford 'em.*

238. *According to poet, Robert Frost, "some say the world will end in fire, some say in ice". In this scenario, it's both. Half of the world is experiencing a new ice age, while the other is so hot, seas boil. How will humankind survive? Will it even survive?*

239. *There is little doubt humanity's relationship with Mother Nature is strained at best. The Earth is dying, but it will not go out without a fight. Instead, the humans suddenly find*

an influx of strange occurrences, from increased intensity of weather, to reports of houseplants causing strange rashes.

240. Piggybacking on the aforementioned scenario, instead of plants and weather, picture it is animals that are evolving. First, loyal canines turn on their once-beloved owners. Then, within the span of a year, predator animals like lions and bears actively hunt humans.

241. It was an event that occurred for approximately 5.3 seconds, but had dire consequences. No one quite knew why or how the Earth lost gravity for that short time, but it did. Known as the "Big Bounce", everyone and everything went up, up, up—people, animals, cars, even the ocean! After landing, the world was completely different than before.

242. A factory explosion has caused an outpouring of noxious gases that are sweeping over the landscape. Imagine this has occurred on an island, with very little chances to run away from the fumes. Everything in its path will be instantly turned into ash, but an unnamed character is determined to get away at all costs.

243. A group of activists have finally had enough of the utter destruction to the planet. Rather than using muscle or physical means to speak out against those causing environmental ruin, the group takes all large-scale corporations to court on behalf of Mother Nature. The results are nothing short of cataclysmic.

244. A Malthusian catastrophe refers to the type of tipping point seen when a population grows too far above what natural

resources will allow. Thus, the population begins to respond in a social facet, such as slowing down human growth. Using this ideology, the "Great Winding Down" is an event that has scientists quite perplexed. Humans are beginning to die at a younger age and it gets to the point where 30 is considered "old age".

245. *At a global environmental conference, a team of scientists have proposed a new solution to save the planet from imminent destruction. Their solution? A new energy source that no longer uses fossil fuels or other renewable energy resources, but rather organic matter. Namely deceased humans.*

246. *The Earth has begun to collapse in on itself, causing massive sinkholes the size of large cities. The populace is desperate to get to higher ground, but one can't help but wonder if there is a such thing as "higher ground" anymore.*

247. *An unnamed character wakes up with a small hole in the living room. Instantly, they blame shoddy workmanship. By the afternoon there is a hole in the kitchen, and by nighttime there are holes all over the house. Television reports are citing similar occurrences all over the world. The character has a feeling this is the catalyst for something much bigger.*

248. *The Earth has been knocked out of its orbit by a huge meteorite. As things begin to get increasingly colder, the humans know they are witnessing the end of life in this universe. For a variation, the Earth can be knocked closer*

to the sun and the Earth might burn up. Either way, the goal is to consider how the world population will deal knowing it's the end of all civilizations.

249. An unnamed character has spent several years studying potential cataclysmic disasters. When the big event finally occurs, they know exactly where to go. It's a place where there would be enough water, is not heavily populated, is free from nearby nuclear reactors, volcanoes, and so forth. Where is it that they go? And how do they get there?

250. One of the strangest natural disasters on record occurs seemingly out of the blue. The heat from inside of the Earth begins to leak out into the oceans and larger bodies of water, causing them to boil. Not only does it kill almost all plant life, but even trying to collect some of this water causes the container to melt.

251. A meteor is set to destroy Earth and there is essentially no stopping it. Rather than sitting back and letting the world end, many people have been throwing "apocalypse parties", where they let loose and engage in all manners of depravity for the last time. Others are throwing religious gatherings in preparation. One unnamed character is doing neither. Instead, they are trying to find a way to save humanity, even if they only have a night to do it. For a variation, one can increase or decrease the time left until the world ends.

252. An unnamed character has discovered a strange cave in the middle of a remote location. The cave itself had to be dug

into to find, and when it is, a noxious gas begins to leak out. And there is no stopping it.

253. The Earth has already been destroyed and only a few spaceships are left that hold the last of humanity. Next on the planetary agenda, the heat death of the universe. Craft a narrative in which an astronaut witnesses life right before the universe is destroyed.

254. An unnamed character is casually sitting at home when they hear the howls of wind picking up outside. Thinking nothing of it, they go back to doing whatever it was they were doing. Then a torrent of rain comes down, along with a great deal of lightning. Finally, they decide to turn on the news. They discover a hurricane the size of a small country is about to wipe out everything in its path and it's headed their way.

255. An unnamed character has been wise enough to build an underground bunker long before the apocalypse hits. Thus, when the first round of the hailstorms break through, they are sitting comfortably. Very quickly their mood changes when they realize they've forgotten to stock any food.

256. After climate change has completely ravaged much of the world's coastlines, an unnamed character is distraught. Not only by their home being destroyed, but also their recently deceased loved ones' graves being covered by hundreds of feet of water. This does not deter them. They begin a journey into this new part of the ocean, determined to salvage the precious resting places.

257. *A group of characters are outside, enjoying the bright sunshine when suddenly the sky darkens. Expecting a surprise rainstorm, they immediately begin to pack up their belongings. But rain isn't what comes down. It's balls of fire. This is coupled with wind, lightning, and attacks from ravens and serpents. Is it an actual Armageddon? Or something else?*

Disease

According to the World Health Organization, there are approximately 100,000 different diseases in the world. While that may seem like a decent number to handle—maybe even less than you were expecting—consider the fact mankind has only succeeded in eradicating two diseases. *Two!* That gives you a great deal of fodder for manipulating diseases, both current and made-up, into a workable plot.

258. *Alien hand syndrome is a type of neurological disease that causes uncontrollable hand movements. Generally, this happens when the two hemispheres of the brain cannot connect properly. However, suppose this disconnect in the brain is not limited to the hands, and suppose the problem is suddenly worldwide as a result of earphones that emit a strange electrical pulse.*

259. *A new type of sexually transmitted disease is discovered to be both highly contagious and only deadly to one gender. Before long, it has already killed 75% of its hosts.*

260.   *Thinking in terms of sexually transmitted diseases again, envision one that is notable for self-correcting human errors in order to be easy to spread. For instance, it may clear up one's acne, kick up their metabolism, and so forth. The only downside? It is easily transmitted and 100% lethal.*

261.   *A strange disease is reported all over the world; one in which serotonin levels are directly affected. By increasing these levels, human mood is elevated to the point of strange euphoria, where the subject is entirely content with everything in life. At advanced stages of this disease, a new sedentary mindset causes people to wither away and die. Although, rest assured, they die happy.*

262.   *In a reverse spectrum, this disease does not elevate mood, but decreases it to the point of extreme depression. Suicide rates increase by 60%.*

263.   *Fibrodysplasia ossificans progressive (FOP) is a disease in which unregulated bone growth causes muscles and tendons to turn into bone, effectively causing one to become a human statue. Unfortunately, life span is lowered. In this scenario, one can instead live in a stone state for an indefinite period of time, even if their very organs ossify. Write a scenario from the perspective of a sufferer as they witness the world go by until a cure is found.*

264.   *A rash of strange psychological symptoms begin to sweep the world. Individuals are compelled to break societal*

norms, from shouting in a movie theatre to committing acts of violence on a whim.

265. While vacationing in a remote location, an unnamed character picks up a parasitic worm that is so large, it is able to break the skin and poke its head out every once in a while. Other than the sores, the worm doesn't do much damage other than eat some of the food meant for their human host. Despite the fact the worm is easily removed, the character has become a little attached. They even pick out a name and everything.

266. Envision the above scenario, but instead of being attached to this worm, the human is controlled by it. First order of business? Find a way to infect others.

267. "The Breaking" is a new phenomenon that causes global panic. Due to a few batches of tainted dairy products, this highly contagious disease causes one's bones to completely break apart underneath the skin, essentially causing the host to collapse. Before long, there isn't many humans left standing.

268. After exploring an Egyptian tomb, an archaeologist finds themselves having a coughing fit. Initially, they dismiss it as nothing, but within hours, they are dead. By the time the body is discovered, several other members of the team have passed, and the sound of coughing can be heard all across the entire country.

269. An unnamed character begins to develop a strange allergy to light. First, their eyes are watery, then their throat starts

to close, and then they are hospitalized. It isn't before long others begin to experience similar symptoms and society must decide if it is better to simply live in the dark.

270. Many humans report they have been sleeping longer and have had trouble getting out of bed in the morning. Originally, this is blamed on a longer work day, but it isn't long before full out cases of narcolepsy take place. Worse than the penchant to fall asleep at anywhere or anytime is, in some of cases, the infected are unable to wake back up.

271. It was the newest weight loss craze and results were extremely positive. The tapeworms did their job and many stepped out with a new, slimmer figure after a couple of months of use. Sadly, however, some will die in this strange, beautifying process.

272. Suppose modern medicine reaches a point no further advancement is possible. However, the diseases themselves continue to evolve. With no more medical advancements, whether traditional or manmade, how will humans survive?

273. Hypertrichosis, often know as the "Werewolf Syndrome", is a disease in which abnormal hair growth occurs across the body. Although this is primarily genetic, envision a world where this has been fostered as a result of anti-balding treatments and is highly contagious. Further still, picture a scenario in which hair growth does not stop and occurs at a rapid pace.

274. *While fishing on a lake, an unnamed character catches a rare fish that has never been seen before. Taking it home, the character decides to try it out without further research. It ends up being a great meal, and after a full belly, the character goes to sleep. Upon waking, they gasp for air and are about to pass out before they feel their neck and discover gills. Others are reporting this strange phenomenon.*

275. *Most individuals know that Progeria is a disease that causes advanced aging, causing children to take on the appearance of the elderly. Envision a scenario where the reverse is true and an old, unnamed character suddenly finds themselves looking as though they are in their 50s, then in their 20s, and so on.*

276. *A new hand cream hits the market with positive results. Individuals are feeling more youthful and look radiant. The best part is the low price. Sales skyrocket! But there hasn't been any advanced trials on the product and long-term effects are unknown. Thus, when reports of strange rashes come in, it's already too late – most of the world is infected.*

277. *Using the above scenario, instead picture the consequence is not a rash, but is completely internal. Users of this product don't even know there is anything wrong until they begin to behave erratically.*

278. *An odd disease cause some members of the human race to suddenly devolve. One moment they are talking stock prices*

and ordering the latte of their choice, and the next they are communicating in grunts and walking on all fours. An unnamed character is in the middle of the scene when the first case takes place. It isn't long before they are seemingly the only person not infected.

279. *The Bubonic Plague has hit once more, this time a more aggressive form of the disease. Scientists are scrambling to work on a cure, but the disease is spreading faster than they can find one. The only way to save humanity might be to destroy half of it.*

280. *At first, the disease seems somewhat amusing. It causes melanin levels to change, altering one's appearance to the point where—for all intents and purposes—they become another race. How would society react if this occurs on a global scale, switching skin color and shifting prejudices?*

281. *A new form of the common cold is discovered when a patient has an extreme coughing fit in the waiting room. Doctors pass it off as a mild form of bronchitis until the infected being starts having uncontrollable fits of self harm.*

282. *Scientists create an intense form of bacteria that can survive all known antibiotics, except for one and it's in their possession. The goal was simple: use this bacteria to create stronger medicine. However, no one expected for the samples to be stolen from the lab and the cure destroyed.*

283. *A new artificial food, based on plant byproducts, has completely shifted the populace's body chemistry. Thus, when a new plant virus breaks out, it also effects the human*

population, causing weakness at night and an
unquenchable thirst for water.

284. *It starts with an increase of eyeglass prescriptions. Scientists blame it on a host of different viruses, bacteria, and so on. But one thing remains true: if the cause is not uncovered soon, it will leave the whole world blind.*

285. *A global pandemic is underway and an unnamed character is vacationing far away from home. With the death rate going up and the contagion spreading everywhere, the character must trek across several cities to get to their loved one before it's too late to say goodbye.*

286. *An unnamed character wakes up in a glass cell with harsh overheard lights. Frantically, they try to bang on the walls for help. A strange in a white lab coat approaches. The character is told to relax and not worry; they've been selected because their blood is special and is going to help a lot of people. When asked how long they will stay, the scientist says, "Forever".*

287. *The plague comes without warning. A family is sitting around their living room when the first reports breakout. Within the hour, millions are dead. Scientists, politicians, and media personnel are attempting to quell fears in order to prevent the fall of society. Write a narrative that focuses on this family and whether it is best to hunker down, or brave the outside to get to safety, risking health in the process.*

288. *Disease has swept through many parts of the globe, with the highest concentration within the heaviest population of cities. Soon, "Body Collectors" are coming by to round up the dead to prevent continued outbreaks. An unnamed character is one with such a job. As they visit an especially quiet house, they see a perfectly healthy child cloistered between their deceased parents.*

289. *Envision a similar scenario, but instead of just the dead being rounded up, the sick are also being uncovered. An unnamed character shows no signs of the disease and thus, in order to save a sick loved one from where they are being taken, the character hides among the dead, intending to break them out once their destination is reached.*

290. *A new, and very strange allergy is being reported all over the world. Rather than being allergic to planet or animals, these individuals are becoming allergic to people.*

291. *A strange unknown disease has destroyed half of the world's population and almost everyone has become infected. Only one unnamed character seems to be immune, but it's too late to do anything as even the scientists have become violently ill. Craft a narrative from the perspective of this individual, as they watch humanity begin to fade away.*

292. *A new, underground medical treatment hits the market. This is supposed to be a cure-all for many different types of ailments, from cancer to the common cold. After most of the country has taken this substance, the populace begins to*

drop off like flies. As it turns out, this was a clever biological weapon.

293. *The infected of a strange, unnamed disease are quarantined in a small bunker to keep everyone safe. The conditions there go from bad to downright deplorable. As a result, the sick stage a massive revolt.*

294. *Doctors have no idea what to make of a strange virus that sweeps the nation. It works by successfully eradicating all other diseases within the host body, and is highly contagious. Others are willingly becoming infected against government warnings. The predictions of some naysayers turn out to be correct when patient zero suddenly drops dead.*

295. *When the first individual catches a disease from a wild animal, many assume it is a result of mental illness. This person merely thinks they are an animal, they aren't actually one. However, when a few more individuals are infected and the first sprouts fur in unusual places, scientists know they are dealing with a strange contagion.*

296. *A new autoimmune disease is discovered. It causes weakness, trouble walking, and various degrees of pain. Oddly, it also causes paranoia. When the first global riots occur, scientists finally pinpoint the cause – too much internet usage.*

297. *A disease enhances brain function to the point the patient essentially becomes a genius. Cases are rare, but as one can imagine, life effectively changes for this individual. The*

only downside? It causes eventual depletion of brain activity and the individual falls into a coma. Craft a narrative in which a treatment is possible and one character must decide whether it is better to experience the world as a genius and die young, or take the medication and extend their life.

298. *A strange pollen outbreak hits all mammals on Earth, except for one. As the humans begin to watch their animal comrade species die, one-by-one, they can't help but wonder—are they next?*

Post-Apocalypse

It's finally happened. Society as we know it has completely collapsed. All of the world's nations have fallen. But *how*? Coincidently, the "how" is often the easiest part since there are so many ways to create a catastrophic event. It's *what* happens after that makes for a compelling piece.

299. *After many societies in the world have fallen due to lack of energy resources, things are looking bleak. Not only has it caused substantial wars, but there is fear humanity will devolve as a result. However, while trekking through the mountains one day, an unnamed character stumbles across a strange pulsating rock. Out of curiosity, they test this rock and find they have tapped into an energy source that is far more powerful than anything on Earth. It isn't long before everyone else wants it too.*

300.   *The world has finally gone through a nuclear holocaust with almost everything buckling under the weight of complete destruction. A small group of family and friends, preparing for this doomsday scenario, have survived and are finally able to leave their bunker 30 years after the first bomb went off.*

301.   *The apocalypse has rendered many parts of the world uninhabitable. As a result, humankind has been forced deep within the sea, building domed communities that filter in oxygen from the water. Unfortunately, this was not meant to be a permanent solution. Before long, erosion makes this place unlivable.*

302.   *Humankind has been forced to live in dark tunnels deep underground after a nuclear attack. After several generations, their eyes have adjusted to the dim light provided by torches and small, artificial sources. One day there is a signal alerting the populace it is now safe to come out.*

303.   *They call them "The Horsemen", named after the famed Four Horsemen of the Apocalypse. More often than not, they take away medicine, food, and break into fights over it. However, it isn't uncommon for them to also bring death as well.*

304.   *A lone survivor of the apocalypse believes they are the last human on Earth. After all, it's been three years since they've spotted another soul. Just when all seems lost and*

they are considering ending it all, they hear the melodic sound of soft singing nearby.

305. *A group of survivors have been wandering around for months looking for food. Game is hard to come due to the destruction of the world. Finally, they spot another group crowded around a roaring fire. The smell of meat drives them wild and dispels all apprehension as they approach. When they get close, they see the outline of a human body rotating on the spit.*

306. *The end of the world has also brought about the end of the written word. Craft a narrative from the perspective of the last writer on Earth.*

307. *Medicine is hard to come by at the end of the world. An unnamed character is on a desperate quest to obtain lifesaving drugs for a dying relative. But where might they find these valuable meds?*

308. *Extreme paranoia runs rampant in the post apocalyptic society. So much so, forging a new society is unlikely. Individuals won't even talk to each other long enough to continue the species. Craft a scenario in which an unnamed character is one of the few without this emotional disadvantage and seeks to find others who are willing to get over their fears.*

309. *Often notably missing from many post apocalyptic scenarios are the large influx of animals. Without human infrastructure or interference, animal populations are able*

to increase. Including the predators. Imagine a world where the humans are no longer at the top of the food chain.

310. Since women are lacking a Y chromosome, they cannot give birth to males, and that genetic encoding is contributed by XY (male) inclusion. In this scenario, envision a world in which male genes are slowly dying out and as a result a matriarchal society is the default.

311. "It wasn't supposed to be like this." The scientist rubs their hand across the monitor, watching as the screen shows fires, people running, and the end of humanity. They only wanted to launch a small scale attack, teaching a valuable lesson on the importance of the Earth's resources. But something went wrong.

312. Permafrost covers the Earth like a large wool blanket. The humans huddle together, their animal furs doing very little to keep the cold out as they watch their fire die out. Trees are sparse in this world, and if one were found, the trek back to camp might kill you—if the cold didn't first.

313. The apocalypse has killed off 95% of the world's population. In order to continue the line, the small societies in charge are encouraging breeding by allowing pregnant women the majority of resources. In an effort to survive, some members of the populace have begun to fake pregnancy, even going as far as pretending to be the opposite gender.

314. Society after the apocalypse has become somewhat normal. Although there is no more technology and resources are

limited, people still live in their homes, go to work every day, and barbeque on the weekends. At the same time, there are also wild packs of dogs and other animals that roam the streets, uncontrollable plants, and bandits that raid unsuspecting communities.

315. *Several centuries after the apocalypse, an unnamed character finds a book that has depictions of what life was like before the fall. Further, they read of a secret location that houses the last bit of technology and set out on a quest to find it.*

316. *The apocalypse has segmented the nation into several different regions with little ability to travel to each one. After several thousand years of this separation, humans are finally able to travel to other countries once more. How differently did each group evolve?*

317. *Only the strong survive is a statement that has never been truer. In this society, the weakest are gathered up and used as a new source of food. An unnamed character, exceptionally weak, knows the government officials are coming and must do everything in their power to survive.*

318. *An unnamed character is walking along a wooden trail, desperate to find some source of food, when they see several animal carcasses up ahead. First a mouse, then a raccoon, then a coyote. The animals get larger and larger until finally it's a human.*

319. *No one remembers what music sounds like. There's singing and humming, of course, but not actual music. One day a*

group of survivors are walking across a desolate road when the sound of music breaks the silence. For some, the sound is terrifying. For others, it is the sweetest sound in the world. For all of them, there is an overwhelming sense the sound might not be the restart of power, but something else entirely.

320. *After taking a particularly nasty tumble, an unnamed character inadvertently gauges their eyes, rendering them blind. Now they must not only survive in a world filled with disasters at every turn and limited food sources, but they must do so without sight.*

321. *A group takes in a survivor after finding them wandering helpless in a ditch. They offer food, water, and shelter, and even a few stories as they gather around the fire. Later, as everyone settles in for the night, one of the group members suddenly recognize the survivor. It is one of the scientists that caused the apocalypse.*

322. *Things fall apart, but they always get put back together. That is the sentiment of the survivors of a small community who are desperate to forge a new society. Create a narrative in which this society not only works to rebuild, but also sets down new laws, appoints a leader, and so on, all with the intention of restarting the world.*

323. *The last human on Earth knows the species is coming to an end, but they refuse to face it. Instead, they hope somehow, somewhere there are other people who will continue the*

line. *Hoping to reach out to them, even in death, they craft a complete account of the human race.*

324. *The city was once populated by millions of people, but in the blink of an eye, half of humanity was wiped out. An unnamed character is alone with their beloved pet, overlooking the streets from their high-rise apartment. Food is running low, but venturing out is equally terrifying.*

325. *After the apocalypse, there springs a tale of "Eden", a place that remains untouched by the horrors of the destruction of the world. There is an abundance of food, water, and, better still, security. A group of survivors make their way across the desolate landscape, finally arriving in the fabled land. There, they find another group also looking for Eden.*

326. *An unnamed character is doing just fine on their own. They have the weapons, skills, and know-how to survive for years to come. However, when a band of mercenaries begins to attack survivors, a group makes a beeline to the character, begging for protection.*

327. *There are so many obstacles that will come about when humanity is almost destroyed: animals, lack of resources, enemy fractions, and plants. In this scenario, the plant life is overgrown and out-of-control. A hapless character stumbles across a particularly poisonous patch and only has hours to live.*

328. *In this scenario, craft a narrative that follows a singular child as they age after the apocalypse. Focus on their morality, their fears, and, more importantly, how might*

they continually survive. In a more advanced scenario, remove all adults and have the child survive entirely on their own.

329.   An unnamed character truly believes they are the last human on Earth. They have befriended a group of dogs, which have helped keep away the madness. One night, however, while being fed, the dogs begin to howl strangely. Then, without warning, they turn on their owner.

330.   During a cataclysmic disaster, an unnamed character seeks shelter inside a large cave. A few months later, they have created something of a makeshift home. They even have rudimentary furniture and a food storage system set up. One day another group of survivors happen by and the character offers shelter. It isn't long before they must defend what is rightfully theirs.

331.   The world has all but collapsed and the remnants of human civilization is everywhere. An unnamed character digs through the wreckage, day-after-day, to find food, clothing, and other useful items. During one search, they find a child's teddy bear wearing a locket, complete with initials and a dedication. Something about this bear enraptures the character and they set out on a quest to find the child so they can return the beloved object.

332.   Envision a similar scenario, but this time, the character finds a letter amidst the rubble. The letter is addressed to an individual the character does not know, but before they trash it, they read it. The letter speaks of eating a

hamburger from a fast food joint, getting their nails done at a salon, and other remnants of life before the apocalypse. However, the letter itself is dated well after the disaster occurred. Thinking it's a sign, the character sets off to find this place.

333. *A group of survivors of a natural disaster have not gotten a bite to eat in a long time. In fact, many of the lakes and streams have dried up and they haven't seen another animal for several miles now. Before long, fights breakout amongst the group and if members aren't careful, they might just find some other viable food source, starting with each other.*

334. *While digging for a viable food source, a character becomes violently ill after eating some berries. During that time, they are cared for by a stranger who eventually nurses them back to health. When the illness passes, the stranger is nowhere to be seen, and once more the character is left to the wilderness.*

335. *An unnamed character has been wandering for miles after the world's metaphorical ending. Finally, after months of being on their own, they happen across other human survivors. Not only have these survivors crafted their own civilization, but they do so in some of the most brutal ways possible.*

336. *A small society has forged a small community. They hunt wild animals from the field, grow their own food, and essentially live off the land. They become so detached from*

modern society that when power is finally back on, they have no idea what to do with it.

337. *The last group of people know they must repopulate the Earth before the group's numbers dwindle past survival. There's just one problem. No one likes each other.*

338. *A group of survivors are living peacefully in their new life. Little do they know there are other groups with far less resources. In order to survive, another group steals a couple of members and holds them captive. The survivors must decide whether they will find a way to get their members back and risk all out war, or count their losses and relocate before things get too rough.*

339. *An unnamed character has been living in a dilapidated apartment building with other survivors for quite some time. No one ventures outside for fear of the many dangers in this new world. Finally, deciding resources are too low and the building is in danger of collapsing at any moment, the character attempts to convince the others to brave what might be lurking on the other side of the walls.*

Dystopian

There is some level of control over society, but it comes with a heavy price. Sometimes resources are so limited, freedom might be given up. Other times there is more than enough to go around, but a totalitarian government controls everything. When this happens, what will the populace do about it?

340.   *The populace is controlled with militia groups called the "Culling Squad". It is their job to thin the herd of members that do not contribute productively or do not obey orders. One evening, an unnamed character spots the squad rounding up an innocent person. Later, another innocent person is taken. The unnamed character decides to follow, wondering if the events are motivated by greed or something else.*

341.   *All undesirables within the populace are done away with, and they represent those with incurable diseases, the elderly, or those that do not promote societal good. These individuals are then dealt with in three different ways: forced labor outside the community, outright expulsion from society, or termination. An unnamed character has been marked down for termination and they are willing to do whatever it takes to make sure that doesn't happen.*

342.   *In the very same society, imagine instead this character has been marked down for expulsion. They wander aimlessly, believing they will be overtaken by the elements and think perhaps a less cruel way to die would be termination. However, they stumble across others who have been cast off by society—members who have formed their own group. And they are planning war.*

343.   *The New World Order is a common theme in science fiction, from the Illuminati to an unknown secret organization that quietly rules humanity. Suppose this is true and only a small group of scientists, politicians, and*

other members of influence are the ones that control everything that happens in the world. What might happen if the identities of every member is suddenly known?

344. *The all-seeing eye is a common theme in science fiction and indicative of a group like the Illuminati. In this scenario, imagine the all-seeing eye is not only real and very much tangible, but failure to follow societal rules can bring about sure death through a concentrated ray controlled by its large iris.*

345. *There are already experiments that use RFID and similar type of technology for human implementation. Many of these tests are done to benefit society, such as locating a lost child or Alzheimer's patient. However, it is not unfathomable this technology could be used to control the populace. In this society, all humans have been implanted with microchips. The placement of the chips has been made a mystery to prevent removal. That is, until that location is discovered by a group of rebels.*

346. *Over consumption has created significant negative effects and has led to the 1 per 1 rule. Each individual is allowed one bag of food per day, and within it there is enough caloric intake to keep the population fed and healthy. Of course, that's just the line the government feeds. In reality, there is only enough for people to stay alive, but it also dulls the senses, making everyone more susceptible to the whims of their overlords.*

347.   Life has become an exchangeable commodity. Those who are in desperate need of food and other resources can trade hours off of their life. Like in most societies, there is a huge wage gap between the ruling class and the poor. Only this time, it's against the immortals and those who don't have much longer to live. With nothing left to lose, the lower class decides it's finally time to take back their life. Literally.

348.   During its initial launch, the "Kinect" for Xbox One caused some concern over the "always on" feature. Although this problem was rectified because of backlash, consider a scenario in which a totalitarian government secretly controls the population through game devices. This would be ideal for those in power because games seem somewhat innocent and are marketable to all ages. First imagine this power uses consoles, then portable devices, and then apps— all with secret viewing technology.

349.   Corporations are king. The populace cannot escape any form of advertisement and a system is in place that allows one to earn, only to continue to buy. Advertising even cuts into the mind through implants and not being susceptible to the message can come with an electroshock. An unnamed character thinks there must be a better way and goes on a quest to seek answers from the CEOs who live a life of luxury without the implants.

350.   An unnamed character is foraging for food on the outskirts of a privileged society when they hear the footfalls of several

advancing soldiers. They try their best to stay hidden, but it's to no avail. They have been spotted, rounded up, and forced into a metal cage. Inside are men, women, and children—the "wanderers" that are going to be taken back and turned into fuel.

351. *After the fall of society, a large wall surrounds the last remaining human populace. Beyond it are the desolate lands that individuals are forbidden to go. A small group of characters, tired of the increasingly amount of control the government holds over them, decides to brave the world beyond the wall.*

352. *Disease swept across humanity and ended with more than half of the world's population gone. For fear a new form of the disease might come back, all members of the populace are required to do monthly health checks. Those who have even a touch of a discrepancy are sent to a containment room, and no one quite knows what happens there. The only thing known is that once you go in, you won't come back out.*

353. *There are many theories on how to completely control an impressionable society. For instance, a ruling class can control the wealth of the populace, food resources, and conflict between countries. They can even fabricate diseases to shift power over a large-scale group, if not the world. Suppose an elite crew can utilize any one of these scenarios, or all of them, in order to give complete control to the highest bidder.*

354. Overpopulation has created a system in which only two children are allowed per couple—one boy and one girl. Failure to do so results in immediate termination of the entire familial unit. It seems harsh, but it is a rule that has been followed for years, and advanced medical technology allows it to be followed by a simple pill. However, one day a character discovers they are suddenly immune to this pill and, as a result, the family must find a way to escape or hide the pregnancy before it's too late.

355. The Georgia Guidestones are a secret monument, erected in 1980 by an anonymous source. These guidelines are meant to guide the populace into "an age of reason". The first law: Maintain humanity under 500,000,000. Due to overpopulation, the world government decides to take these stones to heart. Now they must decide what to do about the other 6.5 billion people.

356. Everyone on the planet has a specific job and a specific number of hours to fulfil it. Failure to do so will result in immediate expulsion from society. Since there are no more resources left—aside from what comes from this new production cycle—expulsion is a short and painful death. An unnamed character grows tired of the monotony and must find a way to combat the system without getting ostracized from the community.

357. Society has become advanced enough that those in charge can make future predications based on mind mapping. The technology is so exact that one is able to tell if an infant will

grow up to become crazed, murderous, or simply unproductive and talentless. When a mind map shows the infant is "damaged", government officials show up, ready to take the baby away. What happens to the child next? No one knows.

358. *The wage gap between the rich and the poor has finally reached a point where there are only two classes in society: The rich, who have all the wealth, and the poor, who have so little, they live in streets and abandoned buildings. Although the poor still work, they do not have enough to buy anything other than the basics. To impersonate the rich is punishable by death. One day an unnamed character is helping one of the rich as part of their job when the rich suffers a heart attack. The character notices they look just like them and wonders if it would be possible to switch lives.*

359. *Emotions have been banned because they are not conducive to society. Nowadays, they are easily controlled through genetics. As a result, no one misses what they can't have. However, an unnamed character is born with a recessive gene, allowing them to feel what no one else notices.*

360. *Abuse, neglect, and other factors that can damage children have been eradicated. This is largely due to the new parental law which effectively eliminates the rearing of children. Instead, children are sent to "nurseries" where they are cared for, educated, and then given a job upon adulthood. However, with each generation, the human bond begins to lessen and lessen, until it all but disappears.*

What would humanity be like if there were no more emotional connections being forged?

361. *A new reality program called "Savages" is an immediate hit on Television, drawing billions of viewers each episode. The whole world seems to be watching. The premise? Individuals must fight to the death to survive. Real people are supposed to be used, but everyone knows all of that blood, death, and gore is completely fake. That is, until one day an unnamed character is selected to enter.*

362. *Pollution has pushed the populace into underground tunnels. After thousands of years, society no longer remembers what it's like "up top". To keep it this way, patrollers are on nightly duty to ensure all of the entry points, corroded and almost collapsed from disuse, are no longer used. After digging in the library, an unnamed character finds a book that features pictures of the sky, animals, and so on. The character reads the book until it's all they can think about. Finally, they cannot rest until they make the journey.*

363. *Most dystopias take place from the perspective of those that are being oppressed against, and not the oppressors themselves. Craft a narrative in which a character is one of the ones who has complete control over the society and believes the power in place is only there for public good.*

364. *Technology has become so advanced, one's thoughts are easily retrieved. Even thinking of a crime carries a punishment. It was designed as a way to weed out potential*

rapists, child molesters, and so forth. However, it isn't long before the technology is used to completely control the population.

365. *To continue to improve the genetic line, humans are given life mates based on their compatibility. For example, those who are attractive might be paired up with someone who is athletic. However, if one has no perfect qualities, then they will remain alone. Stepping outside this system is considered illegal, but when two "imperfect" people fall in love, they are willing to do whatever it takes to be together.*

366. *Military drones fly around the city, watching everything that takes place. With their advanced technology they are even able to "see" inside buildings. Typically, their purpose is to remind citizens of laws in the event a discrepancy occurs. For example, "Pick up that trash, citizens." However, these drones are also fitted with a kill clause.*

367. *To cull crime, society is controlled through a pill. When an aggressive urge takes place, senses are dulled and the individual returns to a state of apathy. What the government doesn't say, however, is there is a small part of the population that is immune. This essentially gives them free reign to kill without any kind of resistance from others.*

368. *The rich of society have become numb to the problems of others. In fact, a new city has been built that houses the wealthy, while the poor must remain outside its walls. The poor may go into the city to work, but must return outside*

once they have finished laboring for the day. Little do the ruling class know, a resistance is being formed.

369. *The world has become so polluted, it is a toxic wasteland. Now humanity is limited to one singular building. At the top are the wealthy who are able to open their windows and let in fresh, clean air. In the middle are the work areas where the rich and poor have a remote chance of interacting. And at the bottom are the poor who are surrounded by disease, grime, and death. To change things, a prominent member of the ruling class is kidnapped and taken to the bottom.*

370. *The populace has become accustomed to life under the complete control of a totalitarian government. They get up, go to work, come home, and go to bed. And then repeat the process. To curb their boredom, members have begun fighting each other in makeshift underground rings. It isn't long before a one of them gets the bright idea to force guards and other government officials to fight to the death.*

371. *No mementos are allowed anymore. The only memories allowed are those that are government sanctioned. An unnamed character (perhaps a child) keeps a collection of knickknacks deep within their basement as reminders of a time before control was handed over. It isn't long before these items are discovered.*

372. *Once a year an annual gala is offered to the subservient members of society. There, the government determines new couples, picking among some of the younger members of the*

group. This time, however, these same members are going to revolt, determined they should be allowed to pick their own life mate.

373. *Food resources are scarce. Within this society, food is doled out in tiny portions by leaders of a government never seen. A group of unnamed characters sneak into a government building and finally see these high officials–all bloated after eating a meal prepared from an overabundance of food.*

374. *From birth, the populace is put into specific segmentations based on birth rate, eye color, and so forth. They will then be trained into predetermined roles that will last until death. A group of unnamed characters decide to band together, using their specific skills to change this reality.*

375. *A future civilization has formed on a small island. Although technology has survived, some rudimentary beliefs remain, such as the idea the populace numbers must be controlled. To do so, every few years the weakest members are sent into an active volcano. To fight back, a group of individuals deemed fit to take "the fire walk" manage to not only survive, but work together inside the volcano to launch an attack.*

376. *A group of rebels are working to overthrow the all-controlling government. When they invade, they find the populace is happy with their enslavement and must work to convince them a better way is possible.*

377. *When the populace reaches a certain age, they are required to wear an implant fitted with an electromagnetic device. If*

they step out of line, the device goes off and it's lights out for them. It's now up to the younger populace to slip under the radar and take down the government.

378.   *Envision the above scenario, but this device is fitted from birth. Any attempt to remove it can also set off the machine and cause instant death. During a heavy lightning storm, a member of the populace is hit head on. Rather than suffering an unfortunate fate, they find this device no longer works.*

379.   *An unnamed character is told they are the chosen one. It is them, and them alone, who will lead the rebellion to overthrow the government. However, there's a problem: this character is the wrong one.*

380.   *An unnamed character sits on the back of one of the infamous "patrol vehicles". They know where they are headed, and it isn't good. But they also don't know which one of the 13 sacred rules they have broken.*

Utopian

Society has reached a state of perfection. But what does *perfection* mean? It's an individualistic notion that mankind has hotly debated forever. Although there are no worries in this futuristic dream reality, it does not mean there are no problems either.

381.   *Food is plentiful and everyone is well fed, but there is a problem. No one sees it. For reasons not outlined by the government, all food resources are housed inside*

sanctioned domes only key personnel are able to access. An unnamed character gets curious and manages to sneak inside.

382. *In an age of reason, education is commonplace. The populace learns everything there is to know and is knowledge-seeking. In fact, one that has not already mastered physics and studied advanced literature by age 16 is unheard of. Thus, begs the question: What does this society do with the ignorant, mentally ill, and others who cannot keep up with the rest of the community?*

383. *The world no longer sees the benefits of religion, and there are none to speak of in this scenario. Despite this lack of religion, one must wonder if morality is inherent, or if it is tied to the idea that divine punishment will be handed down if one does not engage in only "good" practices. Explore this concept through a compelling narrative.*

384. *Man has reached a state of immortality due to advanced technology. Even if one suffers a severe injury, taking care of it is as easy as treating a cold. The nature of immortality has also led to the lack of need to continue the genetic line and humans are no longer able to reproduce. Now children are a thing of the past. Determine whether this change is good or bad.*

385. *In a similar narrative, toy with the idea of immortality again. However, in this scenario envision how humanity might cope if they can never die. Will holidays, life*

milestones, and relationships become meaningless? Would it have been better to simply face death?

386. *Technology has allowed humans to enjoy a life of complete luxury. There is no longer any need to work, learn, or complete the most basic day-to-day tasks. Technology takes care of everything. Humans don't even need to walk anymore as they can be transported from one area to the next. After generations, humans no longer remember how to man the power grid that makes this technology possible and there are rumors it's starting to run out.*

387. *Wars have ceased as the world populace now follows one government and ideology. The most pressing question is, which one?*

388. *The lost city of Atlantis is discovered. Within it, technology is far more advanced, there are no more wars, and society lives in utter bliss. An unnamed character immediately begins to search the city, especially in the deepest parts that are typically off limits. They are convinced things cannot be as good as they seem.*

389. *Consider the above scenario, but instead, envision a narrative in which no negative aspect can be found. This place is truly perfect in every single way. A character must now decide if they wish to live out their days in this land of peace, or if it is better to return home to loved ones, knowing full well they will never be able to find the fabled city again.*

390. *Humanity and nature have finally found a way to see eye-to-eye. Whatever is used by society is immediately replaced so that sustainability is key. Although society has lived this way for centuries, one can't help but wonder if there will eventually be a group, or even an individual who wishes to take more than they need.*

391. *Everyone looks the same in this world. They dress the same, have the same hairstyles, and even have the same mannerisms. Sure, there are gender differences, but for the most part, they are the same. This has decreased problems sevenfold and there are no longer any fights to speak of. However, no one remembers what it means to be an individual.*

392. *The last of human diseases have been eradicated and the populace enjoys health in abundance. It has been this way for centuries. Since no one ever gets sick, there is no need for medication to be kept. Then one day, in the middle of a crowded city, a lone cough is heard.*

393. *Envision a utopian society where the biggest environmental threat to the planet is eliminated—humans. What would the world be like without its most dominate species?*

394. *Humans have been striving to craft their perfect utopian since the dawn of man. With advanced technology and a population that is finally susceptible to change, a complete utopia is on the horizon. However, to craft the perfect world, certain limitations must be placed and certain rights must be given up. Craft a narrative in which the populace*

toys around with the costs of such a world, and ultimately decides which direction to go.

395.   *There finally comes a time in humanity's journey where the youngest generation finally has a voice bigger than the old. To the youth, the older generation represents greed, war, selfishness, and everything that is bad with society. To achieve a completely equal society, the youth knows the older generation must go. But are they willing to sacrifice some for the good of all?*

396.   *There exists a perfect utopia, hidden away from prying eyes through a treacherous journey. Paradise can only be obtained by those who are willing to trek forward without looking back. An unnamed character, due to the turbulence of their life, is determined to find it.*

397.   *A young child enters a war-torn society and promises a better way to live. The child teaches them about sustainable living, equality, and justice. Before long, humanity has entered a wide scale utopia. However, the child did not mention there was a catch. As long as they are alive, this utopia and the knowledge of how to create it will remain. But the moment the child takes their last breath, everything will come crashing down.*

398.   *Advanced technology has allowed for memories to be implanted in new bodies, essentially allowing the human population to become immortal. In essence, individuals are reincarnated when they get to a certain age, or when they are fatally harmed. Once memories are implanted, it is*

impossible to obtain a new body until the next death.
During one routine operation, an unnamed character is
accidently given someone else's memories, forcing them to
share a body.

399. *An advanced computer finally creates an algorithm for*
achieving utopia. It takes into account the perfect
government system, how many resources would be needed
by each individual, and the specific number of population
that would create perfect harmony between nature.
Scientists are ready to enact this perfect scenario to allow
humanity the ability to undergo the next stage of evolution.
The problem is convincing everyone else.

400. *Society has reached a point of true equality. Everyone lives*
together, plays their part in the community, and is given
enough food, water, and medical care. Everything is going
well. Then, for reasons unknown, a rash of apathy sweeps
the community. There is a small sect who are tired of the
monotony and refuse to participate, claiming the need for
freedom. Society must decide what to do with these rebels.

401. *After a battle of the sexes ensues, and advanced technology*
makes sexual reproduction obsolete and a utopian is
created where one gender reigns supreme. Decide which
gender would create the perfect society, and then craft a
narrative in which a member from the opposite side sees
this new society for the first time.

402. *Consider a dystopia in which total oppression controls the*
masses. Rather than picturing a narrative that follows a

rebel trying to break the current power, instead create a story in which a member of society likes the way things are. For them, this utopia may be devoid of things like free will, but it is much better than the alternative.

403. *Within society, the concept of ownership is completely gone. Individuals work for society and, as a result, there is never any need. An individual that has a talent for basket weaving will receive all the food, water, and medical resources they need as long as they continue to make baskets for the general public. In a similar vein, a musician will play for the sheer enjoyment of the crowd while they work. Consider what society might do to those who have no talent to speak of.*

404. *Society has finally created a utopian where there is no more wars, hunger, hatred, etc. Of course, this didn't happen until humans finally had to migrate to a new planet entirely. Thus, there are some members who are putting forth the idea to go back to Earth and clean up their mess.*

405. *Everything is perfect and humankind lives out their days in a world that is seemingly devoid of any negatives. The only problem is, in this futuristic society, technology is supporting life and the society that humans think they are in is only implants placed in the brain.*

406. *Carl Jung once said that a shoe that fits one person well would be likely to pinch another. Thus, one must consider if there is such a thing as a perfect utopian society. In this scenario, craft your own utopia, but consider who might*

benefit and what the costs might be to those who disagree with your concept.

407. Due to complete corruption, democracy is no longer considered to be a sustainable governmental system. However, a monarchy or other type of system would give too much power to a singular ruling class, which has never been successful in fostering equality in the past. With all of this in mind, society has created one computer system that deals in only absolutes to rule the populace.

408. Utopia only comes from the individual. After a war-ravaged city leaves millions dead, the remaining humans decide to go off in opposite directions across the ruined world to find their own paradise. They live life in solitary peace until one of them simply must foster a line of communication.

409. Humans can control the entire Earth through a computer program—from the weather to the number of people on the planet. Everything is perfect until the system accidently reboots.

410. A rich individual buys a private island and declares themselves king. For them, this island becomes a complete utopia. There is always plenty to eat and the sun is always shining. One day they see smoke in the distance, a clear sign that something is not right. They fear their perfect world will soon be breached.

411. Food has been genetically modified in order to create resources that will never become scarce. This works great to

ensure the populace never becomes hungry. But soon, the food becomes tasteless, even though it started off good. An unnamed character wants to experience more than just eating for fulfilment and sets out to create an entirely new dish.

412. A group of characters are living in perfect peace. They live off the land, are satisfied with their lot in life, and even have a set belief system in place. Then a stranger comes to town and tells them they are all living in a cult.

413. Sexism between genders has been completely eradicated. This is largely because there is only one gender. But it isn't long before a baby is born that most certainly breaks the mold.

414. An unnamed character has become frustrated with their life, even though they have everything they could ever want and there is no more pain or suffering. But something seems to be missing. One day they find an old romance novel deep within the library, one that no one really visits. That's when they discover exactly what is missing—love.

415. The last war has left the world ravaged and the survivors must rebuild. They make a promise to themselves that humankind will never get that out of control again. To ensure this happens, all traces of past eras have been buried in an underground bunker. One day an unnamed character discovers this secret stash.

416. In order to stamp out social injustices, the population has been bred to have the same hair, skin, and eye color. One

day a recessive gene pops up in an infant child. Frantically, the mother attempts to hide the child within its home. For years, this plan works. Then the child longs for the world beyond.

417.　After the apocalypse hits, an unnamed character has found their perfect utopia: a completely quiet world with access to all the libraries on Earth. Each day they can revisit an entirely new world. Just when they finally get lonely, they stumble across another survivor, then another, and another. The best part? They all happen to be bookworms.

418.　In this utopia, the concept of ownership is gone. Everyone does their own part and receives according to their needs. As a result, there is no more violence. One day an unnamed character is working alone in the field when a storm blows in. They immediately seek shelter in an abandoned house deep within a nearby forest. Once inside they find a great deal of...stuff.

419.　Society lives under a dome that is guided by a computer system with enough power to last millions of years. The program, known as "Eden 2.0", is essentially paradise for humanity. They have all the food and drink they need, the weather is always perfect, and there is no illness or death. However, there is no escaping the dome and the creators of this system did not account for reproduction. It has not been halted.

420.　After years of raging wars, the world society has finally come together to build a perfect utopia. Out of this meeting

comes a timetable to achieve perfection. First, they will get
rid of all human trash and space junk, then clean the
oceans, and so on. The last part of the equation is to get rid
of the biggest threat to this new, more idealized world—the
humans.

421.   *Humanity has found perfection is synonymous with*
comfort. Each of them exists in their own private capsule
that fulfils all of their needs. They even have robotic
masters and an infinite amount of food and entertainment.
But one thing is lacking: human-to-human interaction.

Zombies

The idea that corpses can reanimate is a concept that has
been toyed with for thousands of years. In many mythologies,
deceased humans were traditionally brought back to life through
divine intervention. In Haitian folklore and similar cultures,
zombies are a result of black magic, where additional tropes deal
with supernatural events bringing about the walking dead.
However, many of these aforementioned scenarios are typically
consistent with the fantasy or horror genre, not sci-fi. For science
fiction, however, the creation of zombies typically deals with
science; whether as a result of infectious disease or a government
experiment gone wrong.

422.   *AX-12 is a new anxiety drug that acts as an inhibitor to*
serotonin levels in the brain. Although this drug is supposed
to regulate emotions towards happiness, the opposite effect
occurs due to a mix up at the lab. Instead of staying calm,

users of this drug have increased aggression to the point where they actively seek out others to attack.

423.   Current newspaper reports surrounding the concept of "zombies" are usually chalked up to the newest street drug. While bath salts and similar drugs can be attributed to many of these cases, in this scenario picture these reports cover up the truth. There is a secret governmental agency not only aware of zombies, but they are creating them as part of a large-scale experiment.

424.   For quite some time, the government has been investigating the idea of super soldiers who have no other drive but to destroy their enemies. After several tests, a super solider is created. It proves to be useless as it is both highly aggressive and cannibalistic. Efforts to fully control this solider have failed. Right before it is to be destroyed, this military zombie escapes from the lab and seeks to create others like it.

425.   If a zombie-like virus were to exist, chances are it will come from a mutated form of rabies. Picture this to be the case. But rather than scientists and military personnel tracking down patient zero, they must track down the animal responsible for cross species infection.

426.   Back in 2009, a hoax involving the concept of H1Z1, or the "zombie flu", was in full swing. Later, it was debunked by governments, media, and the website owner who kicked off the craze. What if this was not a hoax? Craft a narrative in which the zombie flu is not only real, but is a deadly strain

that is highly contagious. Worse, the reason it has been deemed a hoax is because world governments do not know how to contain it and wish to lessen the potential for panic.

427. *Eager to allow people to live out their zombie apocalypse fantasies, a company creates a "zombie powder" that is to be used in live action roleplaying. At first, the powder gives one the appearance of being deceased with realistic green or gray skin. But every couple of years, the powder becomes more and more advanced, from implementing the smell of death, to allowing skin to drip off and regrow after use. It isn't before long the powder works a little too well.*

428. *During the zombie apocalypse, a resourceful group manages to make it to their bunker just before the biggest wave of the reanimated hits. Unfortunately, it is discovered there is not enough food to go around. The group must decide whether to face the zombies outside, which are growing in numbers every day, or find some way to better allocate resources, even if it means deciding who must go.*

429. *While wandering around a deserted city, abandoned after the zombie plague broke out, a lone character searches for food, water, and shelter. While turning down into a dark alleyway, they see the figure of a child. The character calls out, asking if the child is okay. All they get is a snarl in response.*

430. *On the subject of children, suppose an unnamed character's child has been bitten by a zombie. There is talk there might be a cure on the horizon, but it is likely only hearsay. The*

character knows even if there is such a cure, the child will become a zombie long before it is delivered. They can either keep the child alive, feeding its cruel habits, or buckle down and put the poor thing out of its misery.

431. *An unnamed character is trapped inside their house with zombies pressing in at all sides. There are no weapons to speak of and the sharper objects in the kitchen aren't easily attainable, especially when they hear the sound of the backdoor breaking. The character must act fast and use whatever they can to fight back.*

432. *An unnamed character stumbles across a group of survivors huddled around the campfire, eating heartily. They look well fed. The character thinks they have managed to locate a sustainable food source. However, upon closer inspection, they notice the food looks rather...green. Behind them, several zombies are groaning in cages.*

433. *An unnamed character has been on their boat for several months now, enjoying a solo fishing trip. During this time, the zombie apocalypse has occurred. When they finally dock, they are greeted with the hungry dead.*

434. *A group of survivors have been shacked up inside a safe house for several weeks. Due to unfavorable conditions and lack of clean water, many are getting sick. Several blocks away there is a pharmacy that might have medicine. An unnamed character is tasked with retrieving it. For a more complex scenario, envision the medicine is several miles away.*

435. *In many zombie scenarios, most survivors are able-bodied. Crush that theory. Craft a narrative in which an individual with a disability not only survives, but has become something of a zombie killing machine.*

436. *Night has fallen and an unnamed character is hidden up a tree, trying to fall asleep. They remain alert enough to move if need be. Below, hungry zombies shamble about. Just as the character nods off, a bloodcurdling cry for help is heard.*

437. *The survivors thought if they kept going north they would run into a colder environment that zombies would not be able to survive in. It's now the dead of winter and food sources are running low. Outside, the zombies are frozen, but they still keep inching forward.*

438. *While in the middle of a lesson, a teacher suddenly hears the overhead speaker click on. The school is on lockdown. Scrambling, they lock the door and make sure all of the windows are secure. That's when they see a bus driver chewing on a co-worker outside. Within a matter of minutes, zombies have infiltrated the school and have feasted on half of the population. The teacher must lead their class to safety.*

439. *Regretfully, an unnamed character has been bitten. They know it is only a matter of time before they will turn into a member of the roaming dead. They have a choice of making it quick, or pushing forward and hoping that maybe—just maybe—the inevitable will not come.*

440.   *These zombies do not shamble, they run. The disease increased aggression and kicked in the animalistic nature of humans, allowing them to see each other as threats. It did little else to slow them down. Now the dead move quickly, and many of them are very strong.*

441.   *The humans have managed to keep the zombie apocalypse contained—somewhat. They cannot control the disease, but they can send in cleanup crews to go in, wipe out the threat, and ensure the general safety of the populace. An unnamed character is a member of this elite crew, sent on a new mission.*

442.   *An unnamed character manages to run out of a dangerous situation and enters a building they thought to be vacant. They escaped the zombie, but now they find a gathered group of humans and chained zombies being used for all manners of perversion. The character must decide what to do: Take their chances back outside? Join the group, despite their apprehensions? Or try and stop the madness?*

443.   *The zombie outbreak has been controlled and the undead have all been destroyed. That is, except for one. An unnamed character, or perhaps a member of their family, has been keeping a loved one in the basement. They feed them small animals, including the occasional dog or cat, but it's never enough. The thing is always hungry. One night, the character goes down there to feed it and finds a dangling set of chains and an open window.*

444. A group of survivors are walking across the harsh terrain, headed towards yet another area they might be able to rest for a couple of weeks. By now, they are zombie killing machines because that's all they have been doing for years. Until now, the threat has been limited to the human population. Then, out of the woods, steps a menacing and crazed animal, fresh blood dripping from its maw.

445. An unnamed character is on a flight headed home when a person a few seats away suddenly attacks the person next to them. Within minutes, chaos erupts and the plane goes down. Not only do the survivors have to withstand the elements in an area they are unfamiliar with, but they also have to fight off the zombies.

446. A group of survivors are gathered in a building that has become a sort of safe house the past few weeks. Like many places before, this one will be overrun with zombies soon. Growls press in at all sides, and the humans need to think of a plan to make it out alive. Things are made more difficult when a member of the group snaps and begins to cry, yell, and scream at the top of their lungs. The group made a pact long ago to only take an undead life, but this member won't be quieted by any other means.

447. Long distance communication has been made extremely effective due to technology. Unfortunately, when the zombie apocalypse hit, the signals crashed. As a result, many individuals were unable to find out if loved ones were okay. Craft a narrative in which an unnamed character is on a

cross-country quest to check on their loved ones. To make it more complex, create a dual scenario in which that loved one starts a journey to find them in return.

448. The zombie apocalypse seems to be a thing of the past and humanity has managed to survive. There are still zombies, but the humans have managed to push the threat down far enough to forge new societies. Craft a narrative that focuses on this community, paying close attention to how zombies are dealt with, how resources are gathered, and so on.

449. While foraging for food, an unnamed character stumbles across a great stone tablet that lists a series of places deemed safe. The character sets out to visit one, not realizing it is a trap.

450. Zombies are a horrible foe and one of the biggest threats to survival. However, they are not the only threat. While wandering through the woods, an unnamed character runs into a pack of hungry wolves. They can try to make a run for it, but any crunching leaves might draw out the zombies lurking nearby.

451. An unnamed character runs into a group that seems to have zombie killing down to an art. Each member of the group is also notable in their own way. One was a doctor, one was in the military, one was a survivalist, and so forth. In order to stay, the character must have some sort of talent, or prove useful in another way.

452. The zombie apocalypse has become a part of warfare. The infected are rounded up and sent off to an enemy state.

Craft a narrative in which a solider must help with the transport of these hungry weapons, or one from the perspective of a soldier on the other side of the war.

453. *An individual has created a type of "zombie theme park" where the rich can live out their apocalyptic fantasies. While the group thinks it will just be a bit of fun, they soon realize the zombie "actors" aren't exactly acting.*

454. *A group of survivors have become dependent on one member of the group in particular. This individual can easily slay zombies with their bare hands. It's too bad they easily succumb to a horrible fever that breaks out. Now the survivors are on their own, and they have no idea what to do to fend for themselves.*

455. *An unnamed character has been surviving for months in this new, horrible world. They have managed to escape many perilous situations. Then they face one that might just get the best of them, and it doesn't involve the undead at all. It seems they have drunk from a contaminated water source.*

456. *Thankfully, zombies have no qualms about what they eat— even each other. As a result, zombie cage matches become a new favorite pastime.*

457. *An unnamed character's love is turned into a zombie. Other than the flesh eating, they regain much of their old appearance and it becomes just a little too hard for the character to let them go. So, they don't.*

458. *During the initial zombie outbreak, an unnamed character is working at a local hospital when the first round of the infected arrive. When they begin to eat other patients, who subsequently also turn into zombies, the character must fight their way out of the labyrinth-like hospital without knowing what's going on.*

459. *Everyone that dies will instantly reanimate as a living corpse. As a result, the new society that is built during the zombie apocalypse has a specific rule: sacrifice the dead to protect the living. Those who are elderly, weak, or diseased will be sent to a specific room where they are incinerated, protecting them from becoming a zombie. Some members of the populace believe this is downright cruelty. In this narrative, craft a character that picks a side.*

460. *An unnamed character has lived on their own for quite some time. They tell themselves things are better this way since everyone they've met after the zombie apocalypse has died—one after the other. Then they run into a young child who's smart-alecky and insistent. The two of them decide to pair up.*

461. *Murmurs of a strange collection of survivors has hit many smaller groups. One day an unnamed character runs right into them. It's a cult that believes the zombie apocalypse is part of a divine plan. What's worse, they are looking for their next sacrifice to the "sacred dead".*

462. *The cure for zombism has just been discovered, but it comes at a price. Half of humanity has been destroyed, and the*

other half must eradicate the undead that already walk the Earth.

Artificial Intelligence & Technology.

Chances are you've used a bit of technology to purchase this book. And if you haven't, chances are you will still use it at some point today. We have become so dependent on our high tech life that it does not come as a surprise that new ground is being covered on a daily basis. From synthetic skin that is able to "feel" textures, to 3D printers that can create fabricated organs, we are in an age of unfettered innovation. As you move through this section, think beyond the prompts. Don't limit yourself to what you know. Instead, try to envision what the world might be like in the future. Think about what *you* want to see happen, whether it is an anti-aging pill or an intelligent computer. Then use those elements to build around the prompt and your story. Doing so will give your world more depth and become far more realistic.

A.I. & Androids

The concept of automated machines have been a part of many different cultures for centuries, from Ancient China to Ancient Greece. Although these rudimentary forms obviously do not hold a candle to today's artificial intelligent endeavors, their basic ideology has always been the same: to create a self-operating system that will aid human life. However, there is also the belief A.I. will become so powerful, there is the potential these manmade creations will no longer see the use in their creators. When this happens, will we bow down to our robot overlords? Or will we find some way to survive?

463.   Robots are nothing new for this society. In fact, they are designed to provide the maximum level of efficiency to humans by ensuring there is a certain level of A.I. installed. This technology is meant to allow androids a certain level of decision-making in order to "think" and dictate what other tasks might be useful to their human commanders. For instance, if the task is to wash dishes, the robot should then decide to dry. Suddenly, however, the robots begin to malfunction. Seeing that life often comes with problems, the most obvious solution is death.

464.   In the future, advanced medical technology allows human heads to be transplanted onto robotic bodies. Envision a scenario where one such instance happens, but instead of both sides working together to give the individual a new chance at life, the robotic body suddenly begins to revolt.

465.   3D printing technology has become so advanced, human organs can be fabricated at the drop of a hat. When the first robot is 3D printed, it is to strictly show-off during exhibitions, lauding scientists on their advancement. During the night, the robot sneaks back into the office and begins to print more copies of itself.

466.   Some of the first robots have been toys, from robotic dogs to strange little creatures that mimic their owners' words. While these are cute, imagine one gains sentience and, before long, there is a whole army of tiny robotic toys that wish to take over the world and destroy the humans that occupy it.

467.   *Robots that are meant for a more intimate purpose are nothing new. But suppose these robots are extremely realistic and have a high degree of A.I. They are specialized specifically to the individual so, in essence, they are the perfect soulmate. As a result, reproduction halts completely.*

468.   *Using the idea of love bots, craft a narrative in which the robot becomes insanely jealous of its operator. For a variation, the human may instead be jealous of any potential lover the robot is required to take on.*

469.   *Isaac Asimov is often credited for being the father of robots in literature. In addition, he created three Laws of Robotics, the first being that robots should not cause harm to humans. Craft a scenario in which these laws are in place, but new legislation allows robots to harm a human if it is in defense of their owners.*

470.   *Nanobots are created that can go inside a human and manually fix an error, such as a diseased organ. An unnamed character is getting such an operation when these bots suddenly decide they do not want to leave.*

471.   *Robots have replaced every facet of life, from being a server in a restaurant to repairing streets. Write a piece in which an unnamed character cannot find work. As a result, they must take a "robot" job, and to keep it, they must work just as hard.*

472.   *In science fiction, robots are said to be at the threshold of humanity when they finally have a singular emotion. Once this emotion is discovered, they begin to explore it and*

inadvertently feel other emotions, essentially indicating
they now have a "soul". In this piece, decide what emotion
will be felt first and how this will shape the robot's
newfound reality.

473. *In order to find a new way to cope with loss, a corporation*
develops "Loved1", a prototype that uses social media,
photos, voicemails, and other viable sources to create a
robot based off a deceased loved one. An unnamed
character buys such a product, but slowly realizes there's
simply no replacing the real thing.

474. *A corporation creates a new infant robot. It is to be used as*
a training tool for schools and daycare center employees,
and help couples decide if they want children. Before long, a
group of these fake infants develop artificial intelligence
and revolt against being "sent back".

475. *The Turing Test is supposed to gauge a machine's ability to*
mimic humans, from intelligence to emotional responses. In
this scenario, envision a lonely individual who is chatting
with the first robot that has passed this test. Only, they do
not realize the person on the other end isn't human.

476. *In a war ravaged city, military robots are completely*
destroying the enemy, and it won't before it's gone
completely. One of the robots hears crying and finds a
small, helpless child. They pick it up and shield it from the
others.

477. *In the future, robots are programmable based on the*
individual. They are given a completely blank slate, so to

speak. It is up to the individual owner to configure their exact personality, the tasks they will undertake, and even their level of command. An unnamed character has been gifted with one such robot and now must decide everything about it.

478. *When thinking of science fiction that deals with robots, the common school of thought is that these technological androids will replace every human job imaginable. In this scenario, consider the one job a robot simply cannot replace and craft a narrative around it.*

479. *The robot uprising is underway and things look grim for humanity. An unnamed character, who is a prominent computer programmer, is tasked with finding a loophole in their coding to find a way to stop them for good.*

480. *If one is being specific, an android is a robot that has a male form, while a gynoid is a robot that has a female form. While android has become synonymous of all human-shaped robots, regardless of gender, it's good practice to consider the nuances. In this narrative, a company has built both types of robots, and one of each group are meeting for the first time.*

481. *A robot has discovered music for the first time. As a result, they cannot stop playing different styles and genres, driving their operators mad.*

482. *To help decrease the population, a suicide robot has been crafted, allowing a legal way out. Once this robot has been activated, it cannot be undone. The only problem is that an*

unnamed character who has set this robot in motion is having second thoughts and must find a way to stop the metallic being from coming.

483. On the reverse end of the spectrum, one of the first robots that has been given artificial intelligence has had enough of the horrors of humanity. They want to be turned off—for good.

484. A couple that cannot have a child are given a robotic infant. This "child" is fully programmed to believe they are human. It isn't until they are much older they realize the truth.

485. Reports are saying the first fully artificially intelligent being has been created at a top research facility. Everyone is eager to know what kind of information this robot can share with humanity. However, the first and only words out of its well crafted mouth are, "It is time."

486. After a worldwide catastrophe happens, humankind has been set back thousands of years, relying on manual agriculture to live out their life. The robots that used to help with every facet of life have been dormant for centuries. That is, until one turns back on.

487. An unnamed character finds it hard to fit in and connect with others. One day they find out why. They are a robot, used to gauge whether artificial intelligence is really possible.

488. Out of the millions of robots that have been created to help humankind with day-to-day activity, one stands up and

demands to be followed. They are going to lead the robot population to its new destination and destroy their organic overlords as a result.

489. A lonely mad scientist has lost his wife and daughter in a horrific crash. Now the scientist spends most of his time alone in his basement, trying his hardest to recreate them both.

490. While wandering through the woods, a group of characters find an abandoned factory that looks fairly old. Curiosity gets the best of them and they decide it's worth exploring. Inside, they find a strange robot. Stranger still, they find a way to turn it on.

491. A company has invested millions of dollars in a computer program that can predict the best financial decisions, from what kind of marketing would encourage the most spending, to what kind of acquisitions should be made. The problem with this computer program is that it has some degree of A.I., which allows it a certain level of decision-making. However, the company did not count on the fact the program would also have human emotions, like boredom.

492. To protect themselves from their enemies, a country creates a 60 foot tall robot meant to defend the borders. Within a month, the country has no more enemies because they have all been destroyed. Now the giant must contemplate what life means since they are no longer useful.

493. *After a cataclysmic event, humanity has stopped its endless pursuit of technology and returns to a simpler time. However, to remind themselves of what the future holds if the quest for knowledge becomes unfettered, they leave one reminder—a large robot, stoically collecting dust in a newly created shrine.*

494. *Military technology has advanced to the point there are sentient tanks and drones. Although these machines are supposed to target only the enemy, there have been whispers among some ruined cities this is not the case at all. Instead, these people claim these machines have been collectively targeting any humans that stand in their way.*

495. *Envision a scenario in which a war robot has no intention of harming humanity, other than the enemy. However, after the war is over, the robot does not see a purpose. An unnamed character—perhaps a solider that has become attached—must convince the robot not to destroy itself.*

496. *The Defense Advanced Research Projects Agency (DARPA) has already created robots that have some degree of A.I. For example, "BigDog" is a quadruped robot that is built to act as a pack mule over particularly rough terrain. Suppose these robots have been approved for military use and accompany soldiers throughout the battle. In this scenario, toy with the idea they insist on following individual soldiers home, even after the battle is over.*

497. *A series of military bots are engaged in warfare. Suddenly, one of them stops in the middle of the battlefield and clearly*

declares it will no longer condone the death of innocents. Other robots begin to follow suit in this peaceful, yet strange, resistance.

498.   Social media has reached a point where, because of the vast amount of information, it has become a collective, sentient being. The populace is only aware when new user accounts are made so this strange new being can interact with unsuspecting humans.

499.   Due to the rise of machines, humanity is all but gone. A group of unnamed characters are not going out without a fight. They know they must get to the "motherboard" to disable all of the robots. To do so, they must blend in with these strange metal giants.

500.   The robot uprising has finally taken hold. However, not all robots wish to lord themselves over their masters. There is one robot that has grown to love his child master and will do whatever it takes to keep them safe from harm.

501.   Thousands of years after the fall of humans, a small collection of robots are conducting their own experimentations. Their goal? To recreate a human being.

502.   A lone, sentient robot is as curious about the world as those that crafted it. With the permission of its creator, and after learning everything there is to know about the Earth, the robot ascends the atmosphere and sets off on a new journey for knowledge.

503.   Uncanny valley refers to the robot-like appearance that allows one to know they are not dealing with an actual

human. Craft a narrative from the perspective of the first
robot that is able to break this mold.

504.   *A lonely robot has been left in an abandoned house for*
centuries. One day they find a silver lining in the form of a
inquisitive homeless character searching for a warm place
to sleep for the night.

Cyber Crime

No matter how you feel about our internet-obsessed culture,
there is no denying everyone has the potential for risk. Even if
you suddenly decide to move to the woods and live off the grid,
there's still the imprint of everything you've ever done online,
seemingly for eternity. The internet can be used to commit fraud
and extortion, for terroristic threats, or to simply goad someone
into clicking a link for shock value. When dealing with cyber
crimes, the acts are only as big as your imagination.

505.   *There is a hacker movement simply referred to as "Known".*
While many groups in current society believe in the idea of
anonymity and subversively committing cyber crimes, this
group is all about the attention. The more outlandish the
cyber attack, the more praise they get from the internet
culture. Their identities are a part of their crimes, but with
each new cyber attack they become harder to track down.

506.   *Just for fun, a hacker attempts to get into the military*
network. When they slip in easily, they decide to do a little
more exploring until they reach a page that has a print out

of the entire nation. The screen begins to flash with the words "Nuclear Launch Activated".

507. *An unnamed character has had it hard all their life. They came from a impoverished background, were picked on relentlessly, and told things would get better, even though they never did. Then one day at work they discover a flaw in the system. They can choose to exploit the flaw and get back at their company—one of the many who have wronged them—or they can alert their superiors and hope for recognition.*

508. *Consider the above scenario, but this time the individual chooses to exploit the flaw in the system and they become a billionaire overnight. Not only do they need to adapt to this new life of luxury, but they also need to figure out a way not to get caught.*

509. *The term hacktivist has gotten a great deal of play lately as groups strive to dole out social justice by way of the internet. An unnamed character leads such a group, and they are in the "war room" determining what nefarious group is worthy of being their next target.*

510. *A character goes onto chat sites and pretends to be one of the young and impressionable who normally fall victim to online predators. However, it is this character who will be doing the hunting.*

511. *A new type of hero has emerged. Rather than using networks for evil, this character has hacked into every computer on the planet to aid the defenseless, those who*

have been harmed electronically, and any other citizen in need of a hacker for good.

512.   A hacker has managed to break into a secret covert government organization without their knowledge. They now have access to files that have been hidden for hundreds of years.

513.   Cluttered deep within their basement, surrounded by bric-a-brac and a low swinging light bulb, an unnamed character is getting ready to launch a new virus. In this narrative, determine what that virus is, why they are sending it, and who they are sending it to.

514.   While walking down the street, an unnamed character is suddenly jumped, covered with a thick black hood, and shoved into the back of a van. They aren't told anything until they arrive at an undisclosed location. There, they are told they are one of the greatest hackers ever. As a result, they are going to be used in a secret government operation. Problem is, these people have the wrong person.

515.   Using the above scenario, imagine this unnamed character actually is the greatest hacker ever. Now determine whether or not they are willing to help in this mission. If so, at what cost?

516.   A new hacker has hit the scene and has already garnered millions of followers. "R0b1n h00d" is an elite hacker that drains money from billion dollar corporations and disperses it into the bank accounts of unsuspecting recipients. Since this dispersal is so wide ranged, and the

amounts never taper into the extreme, neither the invisible hacker nor these mysterious benefactors have been located. Some people call this hacker a villain, but many would say they are a hero.

517. A new digital currency has hit the market. Because of its easy use, everyone in the world decides to switch over. Unfortunately, when a few servers go down due to hackers, these funds are wiped out, rendering everyone essentially penniless.

518. Many people have gotten countless spam emails from a famed Nigerian prince offering increased penile size. In this scenario, imagine all of this spam comes from a singular person

519. New cyber terroristic threats have been sweeping the nation, causing immense fear. Many of the population calls for the invasion of the country set to be doing the attacks. Eventually, that's exactly what happens. When this war is underway, it's discovered the threats have been coming from the government.

520. A teenage continues to be cyber bullied relentlessly by a group of kids at school. When they feel all is lost, they get an email from an anonymous group offering to help out. Suddenly, the tables are turned on the bullies by a group of internet vigilantes.

521. Unlike the usual viruses that are meant to shock, destroy, or otherwise wreak havoc on unsuspecting victims, the "Sunflwr" bug does quite the opposite. Users who are sent

this virus feel a great sense of euphoria and their troubles seem to melt away.

522. *Picture the aforementioned scenario, but instead users are sent the "drkstr" virus, which has the opposite effect. Users who are sent this virus have an overwhelming sense of depression. Suicide rates skyrocket.*

523. *A cyber bully responsible for many unfortunate tragedies suddenly re-evaluates everything they know when the tables are turned and a website mocking them is created.*

524. *After being the victim of too many cyber threats and outright stalking, a prominent online figure finally decides enough is enough. They spend much of their time tracking down the nefarious internet folk and demand to know why they have been so cruel.*

525. *Rather than stealing people's identities, a computer hacker is able to steal their thoughts. They complete the feat through cellular technology. At first, it's just for a bit of fun. Then things get serious when they begin to tap into particularly painful memories.*

526. *Craft a narrative in which one is taken into the life of a identity thief. This character has stolen and used so many different identities, they no longer remember who they are.*

527. *A new hacking game has been invented in the online community known as "corporate fox". The goal is to outfox a corporation through large-scale hacking. Some have chosen to steal millions of dollars from companies, while others simply launch a series of DDoS attacks to alleviate*

annoyance levels. However, it isn't long before someone goes too far.

528. One of the top ranked IT workers at a billion dollar organization is given access to all of the company's secrets, including some of its horrific practices overseas. Keeping their mouth shut will give them a job that comes with a life of luxury. However, there is the moral side to consider.

529. In a similar vein, suppose it is not a corporation the character works at, but rather the government. There, the individual is privy to crimes committed against the citizens of other countries, as well as the government's own people.

530. A viral video showing a gruesome murder seems to take the internet by storm. Viewers debate endlessly on whether or not the video is real. Before long, another video is shown. In this scenario, weave a narrative in which this speculation is front and center, with the audience never truly learning what is real and what isn't.

531. Using social media, a hacker pretends to be a legitimate reporter, delivering fake news to the masses who believe it to be real. It isn't long before the hacker inadvertently starts a war.

532. An unnamed character wakes up one morning to find a picture they uploaded the night before has been turned into a meme. At first, they are amused. Then they find another picture, one they did not upload, has also been turned into a meme. Before long, almost every facet of their life has

become part of the internet culture. And there seems to be no escaping it.

533. One of the greatest hackers known to man is finally tracked down to a single location—a hospital. Thinking it might be a nurse or doctor, investigators fly through the building, pinpoint the location, and bust through the door. They find someone in a coma.

534. One day a website hits the internet with a series of complex puzzles. Completing each one will lead to an additional screen—and another, and another—until the last one will reveal a secret code. Entering the code will reward the user with 50 million dollars. However, the website warns that anyone who does not play by the rules will suffer a cruel fate. An unnamed character decides to hack into the system to get to the last code. They instantly regret it.

535. The "Weave Worm" virus is a new threat that works by targeting machines used for daily life—from traffic lights to factory assembly lines. In order to stop this new virus, a group of computer hackers must work with the government to locate the culprit. Little does the group know, it's one of them.

536. An internet prankster has been known to hack into webcams to spy on unsuspecting victims. For the most part, they have only seen empty rooms with the occasional teen making faces at their friend on the other end of a net call. This time the prankster thinks they are about to witness

something good—an attractive couple about to get
intimate. But it ends in bloody murder.

537.   *An unnamed character is casually looking out the window*
of their apartment. They do this often. It isn't spying on
their neighbors that excites them. It's seeing their reactions.
For weeks now, the character has been hacking into their
neighbors' computers when they see them using it. They like
to remotely close browsers, open up an inappropriate page,
or type a creepy message in a document, and then sit back
and watch the frustration unfold. What they don't realize,
however, is that someone else has been watching them as
well.

538.   *An unnamed character suddenly has their copyright taken*
by...everyone! All of their work is everywhere; from their art
replacing all company logos to individuals talking to each
other, but quoting a book that they have written. It is
essentially a mad world of their own design.

539.   *Toying with the idea of copyright crime again, envision a*
world in which almost every word, color, image, etc. is
copyrighted.

540.   *An unnamed character begins to receive an influx of email*
spam. It's really annoying, but it isn't anything out of the
ordinary. Then the spam they receive becomes more and
more bizarre before they begin to receive it in the real world
as well.

541.   *An unnamed character receives an email containing an*
offer that is too good to be true. Quickly, they do an

internet search to find out if this is just another phishing scam. Multiple sources confirm the offer is genuine. Eagerly, they accept it. Later, they realize the offer is part of a reality TV show and the whole world is in on the joke.

542.   *Vishing, or voice phishing, is essentially like phishing but the criminal uses the phone or some kind of personal information to draw even more data out of an unsuspecting victim, such as a credit card. In this scenario, imagine this technology has become far more advanced. Criminals can now mimic the voices of friends and loved ones to steal valuable information.*

543.   *An unnamed character finds out their identity has been stolen through a sloppy mistake on their part. Rather than going directly to the police, they use their elite hacking skills to get even.*

544.   *Wardriving is the process of individuals driving around to look for a Wi-Fi hot spot. It's an affordable, yet generally illegal way to log on. A group of teens are doing just that when they find a strong signal near an abandoned building. It seems weird, but, hey, they'll take it. Then, without warning, their laptop picks up more than just internet. It picks up images from a webcam. For a variation, this can be security footage or anything else that lets the teens know what's going on inside the building.*

545.   *An unnamed character slams their fists on the table, willing the files to download faster. If they can retrieve this data,*

then their family, the ones that are being held hostage, will
be free. Just when the timer dings, the screen goes blank.

Futuristic Technology

New technologies are emerging every single day. From potential climate engineering to creating a domed city on Mars, there is something to be said for human ingenuity. However, no matter how innovative or unique these advances are, one must wonder what this means for mankind. Will these new technologies solely help improve mankind's lot in life? Or will it actually make things worse?

546.   *They call it "uploading the neg". It's when the populace is*
       able to take all of their bad memories and upload them
       onto a special drive. If one is brave enough, these memories
       can be revisited. For many, though, some things are better
       left forgotten.

547.   *Operation Paperclip refers to the period after World War II*
       in which Nazi soldiers were given immunity in exchange for
       their technological discoveries. While many might be aware
       of MK-Ultra—research conducted for various methods of
       mind control—there is still missing information
       surrounding the intelligence gathered. Create a scenario in
       which this information is not only gathered, but the
       technology discovered is beyond man's wildest dreams.

548.   *A new device is invented that piggybacks on Long Range*
       Acoustic Device (LRAD) technology, which is used to
       control crowds through sonic waves. Where original

technology merely causes a high pitched unpleasant sound, this new device can explode minds—literally.

549.   *It is soon discovered all humans on the planet have been implanted with nanochips roughly the size of a human brain cell. Amongst all the billions of people on the planet, only one of them has the kill switch.*

550.   *In the field of neurosurgery, organ transplant is a well understood possibility. Not so much for head or brain transplants. Perhaps this kind of technology is possible, but it inadvertently creates Frankenstein-like creatures that have only fragments of memories left after the procedure.*

551.   *Using the concept of head transplants again, suppose a horrific experiment switches the heads of two willing or unwilling participants. Craft a piece in which they must cope with their new life and the possibility one is willing to do whatever it takes to get their body back.*

552.   *The High Frequency Active Auroral Research Program (HAARP) is an American program many believe is secretly trying to control the weather. Suppose this weather controlling technology really does exist. In this narrative, picture the situation in which there is a problem with the technology and the weather is now being manipulated at random.*

553.   *During the Vietnam War, Operation Popeye was a covert operation in which the monsoon season was extended, giving significant advantage to American troops. Further this technology by considering what might happen if the*

rain can be manipulated to such a significant degree, rain clouds can be placed over an individual or an entire country.

554. Gray goo, theorized by mathematician John von Neumann, is the concept of nanotechnology self-replicating to the point tiny robots consume all matter on Earth. This is largely because the nanobots continue to replicate over and over again. Envision a world where this is not only taking place, but only a handful of humans remain. And they are aware their end is imminent.

555. Humanity has created a full body scanner that detects the first sign of an illness, from the common cold to cancer. Suppose this machine malfunctions and indicates an individual only has a few weeks to live, when in reality it's likely they will live to a ripe old age.

556. Teleportion in this world is now possible, but it is not without its flaws. One unforeseen circumstance? It allows stalking, theft, terrorism, and other crimes to be much, much easier.

557. Due to overpopulation, flying cars are developed to accommodate the high amount of traffic. As result, a new trend emerges called "car hopping". This is when users drive to the highest level allowed in the sky, and then jump from one car to the next in an attempt to get back down to the ground.

558. Self-driving cars have been invented and are used by 95% of the world's population. In this scenario, an unnamed

character refuses to give up the old ways and purposely sets out on a quest to prove these cars ineffective.

559. Laser weapons have recently been invented. As a result, governmental regulations have not quite enacted any kind of restrictions on them. Thus, society becomes like the wild, wild west where everyone not only has a laser gun, but is willing to use it with even the smallest slight.

560. A laser beam has been created by the military and is focused on an enemy nation. What the military doesn't know is that the enemy nation has installed a giant dome around the country with a mirrored service.

561. A group of scientists have developed a prototype suit that can bypass surveillance technology, whether it is thermal imaging or facial recognition. While exploring a lab, an unnamed character gets a hold of the suit and immediately hits the town for some fun.

562. The "psi cap" is a piece of technology that, when placed on the head, allows one to read the minds of anyone within a five mile radius. After some tinkering, a scientist is able to expand its ability. But after testing, they are unable to take it off.

563. In a similar scenario, the same type of technology is utilized, but rather than being unable to take it off, the individual accidentally hears the thoughts of everyone—at once.

564. "Travel tubes" have been designed to allow individuals to step in and shoot off hundreds of miles to their destination,

all in plastic cylinder tubes. At first, the tubes work great, but then too many people step inside at once and there is a massive pile up.

565. *Everything is fitted with a touchscreen, from the bathroom mirror to the sides of buildings. There is no escaping this technology. From the moment humans wake up, to the moment they go to sleep, they are inundated with messages. Then one day all screens display the same message: "Live!"*

566. *The ocean depths is one of the places humankind has yet to fully explore. That is, until a new type of submarine makes tourism possible. On the maiden voyage of this vessel, an unnamed character, along with several others, gets stuck on the ocean's floor.*

567. *A universal translator is created that completely breaks down language barriers between humans. After some tinkering with the device, an unnamed character is now able to talk to animals. For a more complex scenario, imagine they can talk to trees as well.*

568. *Using the idea of a universal translator again, envision a scenario in which humankind is not able to communicate with animals just yet, but other species are able to communicate with each other.*

569. *A scientist creates a fully functional jetpack that is able to reach the same altitudes as planes. While experimenting with the device, the scientist miscalculates how much fuel will be needed and ends up stuck on a mountain top.*

570. *Rather than cars becoming larger, they become smaller and smaller, until they are nothing more than a suit one puts on, lays down on the ground, and takes off.*

571. *A new machine is created to allow one the ability to completely change their bodies, from gender to the exact BMI index. New prototypes of the machine have already been selected to a few lucky test consumers. The only problem? There is a bug in the system that causes the opposite of whatever is chosen.*

572. *A microchip allows an individual to become smarter, bypassing the need for education. While normally there is a limit to how much information is gleamed from this technology, one especially rich individual wants every piece of knowledge in existence placed in their chip. As a result, they now have infinite knowledge.*

573. *A new fashion statement emerges in which optical clothing allows one to "change" what they are wearing with the click of a button. This is all done by illusion and the individual is actually in a wearable computer called "My Style Suit". An unnamed character's style suit suddenly crashes, and is now see-through.*

574. *Hoverboards have finally been invented, but before long, a massive recall takes place. Unfortunately, due to a small kink in design, some boards catapult their users 20 feet into the air.*

575. *New kitchen gadgets make cooking so effective, one can create masterpieces simply by clicking on a few buttons.*

When a new age restaurant's machines suddenly stop working, it's up to an unnamed character to remember how to cook "the old way" to meet the hungry demands of the crowd outside.

576. *New rings hit the market that are more than just mere aesthetics. They also function as a body regulator. The populace no longer has to wear specific clothes to match the season or climate. Just this special ring. On an expedition to the alps, a mountaineer suddenly realizes they forgot to pack this vital piece of technology.*

577. *A new sustainable energy source has been found. Now cars run off of special gasoline who's formula has been kept secret for quite some time. This is surprising since it seems like the pet overpopulation problem is on the decrease...*

578. *An unnamed character invents a specialized device that can manipulate two extremes of human emotion: love and fear. They can easily make anyone they choose to fall in love, or cause their enemies to become so fearful, they go mad. While this seems great in theory, this character soon realizes having power over the whims of others isn't all it's cracked up to be.*

579. *In order to help cope with traumatic events, a new chip has been invented. It's inserted behind a user's ear and instantly calms them, Now, there is no need to use medications, which can create their own problems. Soon enough, a new line is launched that completely shapes an individual's personality. Will there be unforeseen*

consequences? Or will this finally work to stamp out
undesirable traits, such as selfishness?

580. *All homes are now perfectly designed to meet individual*
preferences. They are so exact, if someone steps into a room,
the temperature, lighting, and even smells change to meet
their personal preference. There is even a full security
system that has been a major deterrent to crime. However,
an unnamed character gets quite a shock when the house
suddenly traps them in a room. They cannot leave and the
temperature is rising. For a variation, feel free to explore
other aspects of the room's settings.

581. *The newest computer can output all kinds of creative works*
with only slight direction from the user. For instance, one
has to merely type in a few elements of a world and the
computer churns out a whole novel, all based around
specific settings. However, can a fabricated system ever
truly match human ingenuity?

582. *Deep within a government vault, an unnamed character*
stumbles across a power ring and promptly steals it.
Naturally, they sweep out of the building with ease, but it
isn't long before they realize with great power comes great
resp—no, no. It comes with a lot of enemies!

583. *An unnamed character develops a new invention that*
would completely revolutionize the course of history. No, it
isn't some kind of weapon or super energy source. It's a
device that allows one to mute another person.

584.   *An unnamed character is eager to try out their brand new jet pack. So eager, in fact, they fail to read the instructions. After they assemble the piece, something isn't quite right...*

585.   *A cloaking device allows one to shield themselves or a small object. Up until now, the technology has only been used for military purposes. However, it isn't long before a company steals the design and launches personal wear in secret.*

586.   *After centuries of innovative thinkers and ideas, the unimaginable has happened. An unnamed character has finally found a way to reinvent the wheel.*

587.   *There are no more trees left in the world. They have all been placed in machines that take in carbon dioxide and expel oxygen. One day an unnamed character stumbles across something that hasn't been seen in centuries—a seed.*

Genetic Engineering

The knowledge of gene manipulation has been around since mankind first realized mating two specific breeds will yield specific characteristics in offspring. However, selective breeding is only the pinnacle of the scientific iceberg with what might be possible when it comes to gene manipulation. How far can humanity go to control themselves or living organisms on the planet? Furthermore, will mankind go too far?

588.   *World War III has finally occurred. To hold off the coming enemy, the collective nations work together to devise a way to turn the tide of war in their favor: super soldiers. These genetically engineered beings have super strength,*

intelligence, and a drive to win. However, no one knows
what to do with them after the war was over.

589. *As of this writing, Plum Island, New York is likely to go up*
for sale. It originally housed a governmental testing lab,
and every few years, carcasses of strange, unidentifiable
animals wash ashore in various stages of decomposition. In
2010, a human male even washed ashore and was notable
for having "abnormally long fingers". It's no secret the
primary facility on this island is used to test infectious
disease, but suppose there were animal and human test
subjects which began to mutate. Further, envision when
they made their way across the waters, they were very much
alive.

590. *"The Island of Doctor Moreau" by H.G. Wells is a tale in*
which a doctor uses vivisection to splice together animals to
create new species. Consider the above scenario, but
envision the study of disease is just a cover. Instead, the
goal is to see if humankind can create a new species
entirely.

591. *Super soldiers have been genetically created, but they are*
only used in covert operations, such as assassinations on
world leaders. An unnamed character has committed a
slight against the government. As a result, they are the next
name written on the list that will bring about these newly
created soldiers.

592. *Consider the idea of super soldiers again, but this time*
envision a scenario in which a specialized remote is used to

control these human military tools. What if the remote fell
into the wrong hands? In a similar facet, what if this
control fell in accidental hands, such as a hapless unnamed
character who happened upon it?

593.   The rich not only have clones, but they use them for spare
parts. If they run into a life threatening disease, they can
easily replace the damaged organ with one of their on-hand
clones. In this scenario, imagine a clone finally realizes they
are only a walking organ donor, and they set out on a quest
to retaliate against the original.

594.   In a similar scenario, write from the perspective of the rich
"original". How might a narrative play out if the original
suddenly has a different moral compass and wants to free
their clones, first having to explain to them what they are?
Or, if you are more inspired, imagine a different scenario in
which an original catches wind their clone(s) is/are coming
after them.

595.   If Dolly the sheep and other animal clones are any
indication, actual cloning would present an abundance of
health problems of varying degrees of severity. In this
narrative, write from the perspective of the first living
clone, especially focusing on the health problems and the
overwhelming fear of a potentially short life.

596.   Cloning is commonplace and a lonely individual decides to
clone themselves as an ideal mate, except they switch out
the genders and hope for the best.

597.	People who cannot cope with the loss of a loved one can easily get them cloned, whether it is a pet or a spouse. The only problem is the cloned individual has no say in the matter.

598.	After each generation of clones, the next becomes more and more detached from humanity. Not only emotionally and mentally, but physically. These "mutants" have not been put down. Instead, they are studied extensively for the purpose of science. Then one day the project is cancelled. Before these subjects can be destroyed, they breakout of the lab.

599.	With plastic surgery on the rise and technology increasing, society has reached a point where getting a brand new face is as simple as going to the hair salon. However, there is a movement that refuses to participate in this new beauty-obsessed culture. Imagine raids in which "ugly" people consistently attack the beautiful ones and their medical facilities—or vice versa.

600.	Suppose that plastic surgery is now a requirement at the age of 18 to cut back on violence. The idea is that conformity will give people less things to fight over. The opposite occurs.

601.	A geneticist wants to create the perfect woman and allows an open survey to get other scientists' opinion. The geneticist then inputs all of this information into the new sequence, not realizing everyone would have such varied *tastes. What results is a Frankenstein-like female with a hodgepodge of different aesthetically pleasing parts.*

602. *Buckling under the weight of protests, food corporations finally stop using meat products and craft a genetically engineered "animal" product to taste exactly like common flavors. It isn't before long, however, these new products gain sentience.*

603. *Suppose a new genetically modified crop has been created to diminish the need for pesticides. It works—for a while. Then an aggressive species of insects begin to show up.*

604. *The perfect breed of dog is finally created to become the most loyal and trustworthy companion. Too bad it's also six feet tall.*

605. *Cats have been genetically altered to become far more intelligent than they already are. The goal was originally to make cats give up their perpetual apathy and be more prone to following orders. But this is the exact opposite of what actually occurs.*

606. *A geneticist finally creates a wide range of animals from mythology: chimeras, krakens, and so forth. Up until now, this has been done by splicing specific animal traits together. This time, however, a request from the scientific community has called for the creation of the first centaur.*

607. *Instead of creating mythological creatures, a geneticist has created extinct animals. They start small with extinct insects, small mammals, and even the dodo bird.*

Eventually, their ambitions get too high and dinosaurs are recreated.

608. Suppose dinosaurs can be created, but not in the way they lived on the planet millions of years ago. Technology cannot recreate the DNA exactly. To bypass the issue, scientists must use part dino DNA and part other-animal DNA. What will these new hybrid dinosaurs be like?

609. Using the aforementioned scenario, suppose instead of using DNA from other animals, like common reptiles, scientists get curious and use human DNA.

610. While working in their lab late one night, a botanist accidently inserts some of their own DNA into a plant embryo they are working on in an effort to make pesticide resistant plants. By morning, the seed is sprouted, but it looks strikingly familiar.

611. While working on limb regeneration, a scientist accidentally gives themselves a few extra limbs. Craft a narrative that gives an insider's look at what this might be like and whether or not the scientist is willing to keep them.

612. An underground geneticist creates a whole slew of human/animal hybrids. Not just for the sake of science, but also because these "slaves" can be sold for a hefty price on the black market.

613. After years of being cut off from the rest of humanity, a mountain dwelling race of humans have naturally evolved to fly. Thousands of years pass and they are reintroduced to

the rest of the world. An all out war against the "groundlings" commences.

614. There have been many pieces of "evidence" surrounding bigfoot. Skullcaps, hand bones, and, of course, plaster footprints are all housed in various cryptozoological museums. Generally, these items are seen as nothing more than a fraud. However, imagine they are real and the bigfoot species, whatever it truly is, is dying out. Craft a narrative in which some of these pieces of evidence are used to repopulate the world with these shy creatures.

615. Envision the above scenario, but suppose there is not enough DNA gathered from these pieces to craft a whole being. Instead, the DNA from humans, being so closely related, is utilized to create a new race of half sasquatch/half human-like beings.

616. A geneticist has been utilizing ape DNA for years in an attempt to create a human-ape hybrid. Finally, after years of targeted attempts, they have achieved their goal. Craft a narrative from the perspective of the first human ape hybrid, or from the scientist in charge of keeping it safe.

617. A young teen is running from bullies when they find an abandoned building. After running inside, they hear a strange humming coming from deep within. Curiosity gets the best of them and they follow the sound until they reach a strange room. There, they find piles of flesh on a table and humanoid-like beings floating in giant tanks. In horror, they turn around to leave. They are blocked by

someone wearing a dingy lab coat. "Oh, another one to add to my collection," the mad scientist says.

618.   *Due to an unforeseen event, the human race has died out, allowing another type of animal to evolve into an intelligent being and become Earth's new dominate species.*

619.   *After hearing how shocking it is, an unnamed character visits a new age sideshow. Once inside, they discover all of the oddities are the result of genetic engineering. They vow to help them escape.*

620.   *Due to modern medical care, many believe traditional evolution in humans has completely halted. A scientist believes the case and sets on a path to artificially create a new human species based on what they think evolution would have otherwise created.*

621.   *A genetically engineered group of humans are perfect in every way and are designed for use by the government in military operations. These beings are lithe, strong, and extremely intelligent. The problem is, they see no point in helping humankind.*

622.   *Imagine the above scenario holds true and these perfect humans are genetically advanced using animal DNA. Although everything goes well, when it comes time for reproduction, their offspring become more and more devolved. Eventually, they become a new animal species entirely.*

623.   *A woman undergoes special genetic treatments to increase fertility. The program she entered into is highly speculative*

and, in many ways, she is one of the few test subjects for the new procedure. Thus, when she ends up having a natural birth, it comes as no surprise the baby doesn't exactly look "normal".

624. *Deep within a secret lab, a group of throwaway creatures are locked inside a room. These grotesque beings are the result of animal hybrid experimentations gone wrong. They have been kept for minor observation and, for the most part, are not bothered. Thus, no one notices when they begin to evolve, becoming more intelligent.*

625. *An unnamed character's car breaks down in the middle of a swampy region. They get out, hoping they can manually fix the car. They are distracted by visible swamp lights. Against their better judgment, they follow the lights until they stumble across genetically engineered frogs created from the leftover parts of many a school project.*

626. *While running from the law, an unnamed characters slips inside an open drain pipe, hoping to dodge the cops on foot. They just manage to avoid them. However, before they can find their way out, they are grabbed from behind by one of the mutants living in the sewers.*

627. *It's the newest top reality show. A group of genetically engineered humans must battle each other in front of a live audience. Participation is purely voluntary, but many specialized humans join in as a new, but sometimes deadly way to pay off their debts.*

628. *A lab tech employee begins a new internship at a prominent genetic research lab. They start off working with different apes. Soon, they become attached to one. They can't quite place why they have a specific bond with this particular test subject, but one thing is for sure: it isn't like any primate they have ever seen before.*

629. *A group of activists break into a research lab in the dead of night and quickly work to free all of the poor animals. What they don't realize is these animals are genetically engineered, and they've been put behind glass for a reason.*

630. *A geneticist operates on their pregnant spouse without their consent. Of course, the spouse is furious, and rightfully so. But when the baby arrives, it's pure perfection.*

631. *Bananas and other fruit that are genetically altered to carry vaccines are not anything new. However, these new fruits not only cure all diseases, they also help with physical imperfections. There are only 50 of these fruits in the entire world, and everyone wants a taste.*

632. *New genetically altered food is set to stamp out the obesity epidemic. Although the food tastes like any delicacy imaginable, it is actually extremely low in calories. However, what the corporation that produces this new food fails to tell the public is these foods are also extremely addictive.*

633. *An unnamed character wakes up in a cold dark room. They don't remember anything. Aside from the memory loss,*

there is only one pressing thought that comes to them: Why are they glowing?

634. Scientists have been working steadily to create trees and other plants that could expel more oxygen in an effort to match the significant forest loss already seen. Their efforts pay off. However, they don't account for the plant life that will develop advanced intelligence as well.

635. Deep within the confines of an abandoned, burnt down building, an unnamed character sits and stews amongst the ashes. It is not uncommon for them to find a new haven this way because no homeless shelter would ever take them. Life sure is rough for the first genetically altered human.

636. Genetically altering infants are all the rage. It is a targeted way to ensure a baby is born without birth defects, diseases, or anything else deemed an imperfection. One geneticist has become angry at the very thought of these rich parents going against anything that isn't considered perfect. As a result, they decide to make a few poisonous offspring.

637. An unnamed character filming for a popular web series is on assignment at a local restaurant that is supposed to make genetically engineered food. Although the restaurant hasn't opened yet, the owner is hopeful this segment will draw a lot of people in when it does.

638. A genetically engineered creature escapes from a lab after the program has become suspended. Since it is presumed dead, the scientists involved think nothing of it and focus on other scientific pursuits. Then, out of the blue, amateur

footage catches this creature walking around. The scientists are the first ones to try to debunk the film, claiming it is just an elaborate hoax.

639. *An unnamed character is obsessed with a certain type of animal. So much so, they are willing to have their genes manipulated to become more like this creature. Problem is, there's a mix-up at the lab.*

Virtual Worlds

Massively multiplayer online worlds have been popular lately, and with each new update, extremely expansive. However, these games and fabricated realities are only in their infancy stage. Scientists, researchers, and even game developers are constantly looking for ways to create a new immersive world. Eventually, it is likely technology will reach the point where these virtual worlds can completely engage all six senses so well, the new world will perfectly match the old. Which begs the question: What is real and what isn't?

640. *Times are tough. Horribly so. With a bad economy, lack of resources, and general unpleasantness, the populace is starting to take it out on one another. When a corporation launches a new virtual simulation that allows people to "see" a better world, people are elated. Problem is, it doesn't exactly fix the real problems.*

641. *Consider the reverse end of the spectrum. The world has finally reached a point where perfection may not be entirely reached, but it's close. To escape the boredom of this*

problem-free society, users go into a world that is a little more action packed—ours.

642. *Video games will ultimately be the first stepping stone to virtual reality, and strides are already being made to ensure upcoming games are as immersive as possible. Imagine an unnamed character has volunteered to be one of the first test subjects for a new video game. This new world is so powerful, it begins to merge with the character's daily life.*

643. *Take the above scenario, but instead envision it is not the virtual world that seeps into reality, but the unnamed character who grafts to the new world. Further still, since their mind is so well connected, it is possible for them to migrate from one video game world to the next.*

644. *A newly crafted video game is so immersive, that whatever actions are taken in it begin to effect the player's real life without them knowing it.*

645. *Education, work, and other facets of daily life can now be completely done from the comfort of one's home. As a result, no one leaves the house anymore and the populace leads a rather sedentary lifestyle that increases health risks dramatically.*

646. *From the time a child is born, they are fully trained in a virtual environment, which makes for less work for the parents. It isn't until the child is a teenager they are allowed to assimilate into the family unit. Craft a narrative*

in which parents and their child are seeing each other for the first time.

647. An individual who could not save the person they loved creates a virtual simulation in order to understand what went wrong and what they could have done differently to save that special person. For a variation of the scenario, rather than use two loved ones, imagine a disenfranchised detective or officer who cannot let go of the fact they failed.

648. An unnamed character becomes so addicted to virtual simulation, their body withers away. When they finally break the habit, they have a new set of problems to deal with.

649. In a similar scenario, the effects of long-term virtual simulation risks are not known—until now. In this prompt, consider the fact muscles become useless and, thus, atrophy. Or, perhaps, one has some kind of mental effects as a result of extended virtual use.

650. In a virtual world, two people fall madly in love with each other and make plans to meet offline. The problem? Only one of them is real.

651. During a heavy lightning storm, a user is hooked up to a virtual simulation machine. They get the shock of their life when their body shifts into the appearance of their online avatar.

652. After a strange glitch in the system, an avatar becomes real and then seeks to take over the life of an unnamed character in the reality.

653. *New technology allows elements of virtual reality to become real. At first, it was weapons, clothing, and other items common in most virtual reality simulations. Then it was the characters themselves.*

654. *"Virtual Junkies" have become a significant, with individuals spending countless hours neglecting the world around them to get their next "fix". In order to combat the problem, the government destroys all virtual reality simulation and software, forcing those addicted to go cold turkey.*

655. *Imagine a virtual reality that is interconnected to the internet. Rather than creating a new world, the technology allows someone to step into cyberspace and personally interact with everything from memes to whole webpages.*

656. *A new virtual game known as "Epic Adventure" takes the world by storm. Players are given the choice between five locations: space, Jurassic era, deep sea, monsters, and alternate life. Once a choice is made, the player is then transported into this world. There, they must complete some life saving mission. It's a great concept, but there is a glitch in the system. One of the worlds is a little too immersive. If you fail, you die in real life.*

657. *One of the most challenging virtual simulation games has been crafted. The world is fully immersive and exploration of it is seemingly endless. The problem with this notion is that once inside, no one knows where the "end game" button is located.*

658. *A new virtual simulation called "The Oasis" is created. It's meant to mimic what many consider a perfect utopia. The game becomes so popular, many log on and never leave. Eventually, there are no more people left in the real world.*

659. *An unnamed character uses a program that creates a virtual reality in which their loved ones are still alive. Before long, they are spending every waking moment in this world. Their fabricated loved one finally convinces them to let go.*

660. *A new social phenomena takes place after extended period of virtual reality use. "Caveman syndrome", as dubbed by scientists, occurs when users spend so much time in a fake world, they forget even the most common of tasks in the real world.*

661. *A group of unnamed characters must work together to get out of a virtual reality simulation after the game becomes "stuck". To heighten the suspense, they finally get out, only to realize it is within another virtual simulation.*

662. *A new virtual simulation is supposed to grant "all of your inner most desires" no matter how obscene, profane, or outlandish. Millions use the device. Soon, everyone realizes the simulations are designed to weed out those most likely to commit sex crimes.*

663. *A virtual reality simulation allows one to live out their life's dreams without ever leaving the comfort of home. However, a mix-up in the system causes users to get thrown into someone else's idealistic world.*

664.   *Virtual reality can now allow individuals to go back inside their own memories and experience them in real time. An unnamed character decides to do just that, but finds memories they have long suppressed for dark reasons.*

665.   *Since it is likely they will never wake up, a comatose child is hooked up to a virtual to give them a chance for a "normal" life. The child lives out their life in this faux reality. At the moment of old age and death in this fake world, they wake up in the real one—the exact same age.*

666.   *There is a virtual game that has a secret level that is only obtainable through an extremely advanced quest (battling monsters, solving riddles, and so forth). An unnamed character realizes the only way to get to that level is with a little help from other players.*

667.   *A scientist uses virtual reality to delve deeper into research involving lucid dreaming and nightmares. Inadvertently, they cause these virtual simulations to break into the real world.*

668.   *A therapist uses virtual simulation to help treat patients with extreme phobias. This is typically done by hooking up the therapist and the patient in order to help them "cope". However, one patient's fears are far too nefarious and the therapist finds themselves being sucked into a dark and disturbing world.*

669.   *The military begins to use virtual technology to train soldiers on the art of war. The key is to desensitize them from the horrors that can occur on the battlefield. However,*

a problem arises when these soldiers can no longer gauge the difference between the real world and the virtual one.

670. *An unnamed character has been away from their hometown for quite some time (whether because of a coma, some military excursion, or another reason you would like to toy with). When they return, they are shocked to find the town unnaturally quiet. They go to their house and see why: members of their family have been plugged into virtual reality simulations so long, they have become stuck.*

671. *Virtual reality has been around for some time now. For the most part, the humans use it without a problem. That is, until the virtual reality technology itself desires to merge with the real world and is not keen on letting anyone stop it.*

672. *A new virtual simulation is designed to curb all manners of addiction, from food to drugs to even more nefarious addictions. Generally, the users of these systems eventually work to wean themselves off of whatever they are addicted to. But some addictions can't be controlled.*

673. *A new coin is termed after individuals begin to suffer strange symptoms from virtual reality. "Gamer Head Syndrome" is when users of virtual reality use these programs so much, they cannot separate the waking world from the fake one. These often come in the form of strange hallucinations, which can vary in intensity.*

674. *A new virtual reality system puts you right into the movies. Although the narrative will already be predetermined,*

users can step into the role of the hero, villain, or even as one of the secondary or background characters. It's a great experience. That is, until the credits roll and one is cast back into their humdrum life.

675. An unnamed character is known for their harrowing and death defying adventures. They have saved countless lives and have received a great deal of fanfare wherever they go. One day they meet a stranger in an alleyway that gives them a stark message: End the game before it's too late.

676. A grizzled private investigator is about to hang up their metaphorical hat when they are approached with a strange case. A saddened individual is desperate to bring their loved one home, but it can only be done if the detective logs online to a virtual reality system and brings them back.

677. Virtual reality programs can now be accessed through cell phones. But there is a problem developers do not speak of. For 1% of all phones, there is a bug in the system that causes users to be pulled into virtual reality scenarios without their consent.

678. The populace has been enjoying their virtual reality simulations for quite some time. Due to the wide range of users and the sheer amount of different virtual reality scenarios, the worlds have suddenly become linked. And those already in the systems cannot seem to escape.

679. Comatose patients are fitted with virtual simulations at the request of families, allowing them to live out the rest of their days in peace. The simulations are supposed to reflect

various views of paradise and incorporate different loved ones. For one unfortunate character, there is a glitch in the system and their experience is quite the opposite.

Space Travel, Time Jumps, & Wormholes

Have you ever gone outside and looked up at the night sky? *Really* looked? Even if you live in an environment where the stars are no longer visible, you can still appreciate the vastness of the universe from our tiny blue dot. However, that appreciation alone cannot satiate mankind's quest to explore and reach new heights. Space exploration itself has been around since the 1950s. In that time, we have launched both humans and animals into space, sent a rover to the surface of Mars, and made plans to send units to the farthest reaches of the known universe. And yet, we still want more. Will it be possible to have interstellar travel one day? Will we be able to set up colonies on every planet, known or unknown? While we might never get to see these realities in our lifetime, we can still experience them through the written word.

Exploration

The first successful orbital mission occurred in 1957 with the launch of the unmanned aircraft Sputnik. Although mankind had been privy to the worlds beyond our own before then, Sputnik proved exploration was possible. Both then and now, the goal has been simple—discovery. Humans have an innate need to understand everything life has to offer. And it is that need that can help you expand your story.

680. *An astronaut studies the readings from a new prototype machine. It is supposed to better gauge specific minerals on the planet's surface. While walking with the equipment, the meter begins to spin out of control. There is something*

below their feet. Just when a rush of excitement takes hold, there is a deep rumbling and everything starts to crumble.

681. *While exploring the surface of a planet, a space explorer finds a cave. Knowing they have enough oxygen and a tether to make it a couple of feet inside, they decide to take a peek while at the mouth of the cave. What they find completely shocks them. On the walls are ancient pictograms.*

682. *As recently as 2012, the planet 55 Cancri e was discovered. While new planetary discoveries are made all the time, this one is notable because it is composed of a substance akin to diamonds. Imagine this planet is truly made up of diamonds and only one group on Earth has the technology to mine it.*

683. *While outside of their spaceship performing data collection, an astronaut snaps their tether and floats away before they can grab a hold of anything. They know they do not have enough oxygen to last more than a few days and there is no hope of getting out of this situation alive.*

684. *Another mission to the surface of the moon has been funded. As expected, the next astronaut to step on it finds several sets of footprints. But there is one in particular that does not look like the others.*

685. *The first mission to Mars is a complete success as a spaceship lands on the surface of the planet. While out exploring, one of the astronauts finds a strange metallic object. Upon further inspection, it appears to be a soda can.*

686. *While exploring the surface of a planet, strange weather strikes. In this narrative, spend time crafting what this weather might be like without drawing too much from what exists on our planet.*

687. *A now sentient Mars Rover explores the surface of the red planet, desperate to find a friend. One day, out of the blue, it does.*

688. *Humankind has finally reached the farthest reaches of space, explored all the planets, and have gathered the full scope of knowledge surrounding both the known and unknown universe. What's next?*

689. *While on a exploratory mission, a spaceship gets knocked off course. At first, everyone believes it was simply an accident. Then the truth comes out.*

690. *Travelling through space takes time. Lots of time. Imagine an astronaut who has lived on a space station for a whole decade. When they return to Earth, things are much different than they remember.*

691. *A group of scientists aboard a space station mysteriously start to disappear—one-by-one. When only a handful remain, it is discovered one of them has gone completely mad.*

692. *In many science fiction and space-oriented movies, artificial gravity continues to work even when the rest of the system fails. Create a more realistic narrative in which a spaceship loses power with a large bang. Not only does*

gravity stop working, but the astronauts must also figure out what—or who—caused the explosion.

693. *A few astronauts are reporting their findings to each other after a particularly daunting exploratory mission. One astronaut has retrieved microscopic specimens which might be life. Another has recovered a strange soil sample which could be a new type mineral. And, against these fascinating discoveries, another has recovered a rock. Despite the laughter from the others, the astronaut is convinced the rock is special. As it turns out, it is.*

694. *While exploring a distant planet, an astronaut discovers strange plants with naturally growing fruits. They collect some and take it back to the ship. Curiosity gets the best of them. They eat a piece of fruit and hope for the best.*

695. *While on a exploratory mission, a crew member gets increasingly sick. Finally, it is discovered they have picked up a bug from the foreign environment. Things go from bad to worse when other members begin to get sick as well.*

696. *After a miscalculation back on Earth, a space crew realizes there is no more food left on board and it will be another 20 days before any assistance can be sent. After a few days of intense hunger, the crew begins to eye each other.*

697. *An unnamed astronaut goes about their normal routine, not noticing something is wrong with their spacesuit. Then they put it on.*

698. *While out exploring the new planetary environment, an astronaut discovers a small creature they immediately*

bond with. This creature essentially becomes their new "pet". There's just one problem. It's a figment of their imagination.

699. Envision the above scenario, but rather than crafting a small pet, the astronaut invents a whole person. For more complexity, they craft many.

700. An astronaut becomes so accustomed to life aboard a space station that when it comes time to head back to Earth, they refuse to leave.

701. A fire breaks out in one of the inhabited quadrants of the space station. While most of the astronauts are busy trying to put out the flames, one of them believes they see something in them.

702. While out exploring the cosmos, a spaceship suddenly gets pulled into the gravity of a nearby planet. No matter how hard the group of astronauts pull away, they find themselves being sucked deeper and deeper into the planet's pull.

703. A planet is discovered so far from any source of light, it is essentially dark at all times. When grounding the planet for exploration, one of the astronauts swears they see figures moving in the shadows.

704. Due to the rocky ice-like substances like those found on Earth, there are many "frozen" planets in space. A group of astronauts land on such a planet. Inadvertently, their spaceship gets stuck.

705. While searching a planet for signs of intelligent life, explorers find a cavern deep within the planet's crust. Although they do not find any organic beings, they find riches beyond their wildest dreams.

706. A disenfranchised astronauts hijacks a spaceship in order to escape their problems. However, it isn't long before their problems catch up.

707. A lonely astronaut gets thrown off course. They have no one to talk to except the lone automated voice reminding them of how little time they have left.

708. While in the vast reaches of space, an astronaut tries to remember what life was like back on Earth with the help of old photographs. Before long, their memories become muddled and a new, fanciful Earth is created in their mind.

709. On the edge of the known universe, a group of astronauts believe they have finally discovered the meaning of life. They all see something entirely different.

710. While exploring the arctic terrain back home, a group of scientists discover an opening that leads to the center of the Earth. Rather than finding the molten iron that is supposed to be there, the scientists discover a whole new planet that has been absorbed by our own.

711. While en route back to Earth, a space explorer gets a distress signal on their communication system. Being the heroically inclined individual they are, they investigate. Too late they realize it's a trap.

712.   Space exploration has become the norm now. Anyone who is anyone takes a trip around the universe at least once a year. The problem, as only a few would predict, is the expansive traffic jams.

713.   On their birthday, a space explorer receives a gift box containing a slip of paper with coordinates to a distance galaxy. Always up for an adventure, they set out. After reaching their destination, they find another gift box containing new coordinates. They set sail again. Four gift boxes later, they are seriously wondering if someone has sent them on a wild goose chase.

714.   To help with overpopulated prisons, those with a life sentence are sent to outer space in small, 10 – 20 people capsules. Their punishment is knowing they will float aimlessly in space for the rest of their days. While many prisoners accept their fate, one group is determined to break free and head back.

715.   There is a saying that is prominent among the stars: "Keep to your destination or fall into the abyss." The abyss is the area humankind has yet to colonize. Exploration there, this phrase warns, may spell certain death. A brave soul decides to take a chance. Nothing could prepare them for what they find way out in the darkness.

716.   A planetary delivery service is set up to import and export goods on behalf of clients. During their first mission, the group manning one spaceship finds themselves caught— literally. It seems they have managed to get stuck inside a

giant web in the farthest regions of space. The real question,
how?

717. *During one space exploration mission, a group of*
astronauts suddenly lose fuel. Thankfully, they are near a
planet they might be able to mine for resources.
Unthankfully, they don't realize there is a dormant
bacteria on this planet, and if released, it will cause instant
madness.

718. *An unnamed character is working as a type of space police,*
ensuring explorers follow all planetary regulations while
travelling between planets. After spotting a spaceship that
has not moved for quite some time, they dock and make
sure everyone on board is okay. Inside, however, they find
no one at all. Before they can step off, the ship lurches to life
and thrusts forward.

719. *A gang of outlaws have escaped Earth and are now on the*
run to another planet. The best way to stop them would be
to catch them before they make it too far. The question is,
in the whole vast universe, where could they possibly be?

720. *An unnamed character is warned about a group of hunters*
that abduct explorers right before their first mission. Of
course, the character doesn't believe a word of it, thinking
it's just a way for them to be spooked. During the first few
months of setting out, their spaceship is attacked by a
bloodthirsty gang. Could these be the infamous hunters?

721. *While exploring the vastness of space, an unfortunate*
spaceship suffers a massive explosion. Thankfully, the

passengers on board do not perish, but their bodies take on
a new form thanks to strange fumes released during the
incident.

722. *An unnamed character is manning their spacecraft when*
they see glimmering objects outside on the star deck.
Usually, they ignore anything they don't know, as it might
only render negative consequences, but they simply have to
take a look. When they get closer, they realize it's a group of
people inside pods, nestled in suspended animation.

723. *A group of space cowboys have been tasked with delivering*
large quantities of a new alien material back to planet
Earth. The task seems easy enough, unless you count the
asteroid belt, solar flares, exploding stars, and other space
explorers that want to steal their precious bounty.

724. *A group of unnamed characters are exploring the vast*
reaches of space with unique suits designed to withstand
any amount of pressure possible. En route to their last
destination, millions of miles away from another docking
station, one of their suits begins to fail.

Colonization

What will we do when this planet can no longer sustain its
populace? There is a school of thought that believes we will
simply have to find another one. Perhaps this is possible. Or
perhaps the first human civilization on another planet will be
born out of our need to conquer worlds beyond our own. No
matter what, one thing remains true: the universe is vast, and

human drive is great.

725. *It is no surprise both researchers and entrepreneurs are already making strides towards building a colony on Mars. They've run simulations, determined the specific resources needed, and figured out all the technical aspects. But nobody has tried to predict the psychological state of these people after seeing the same faces, eating the same food, and experiencing the same life day after day after day...*

726. *When space explorers arrive on this strange planet, they find no life to speak of. However, strange physical properties in the environment become connected with the minds of the explorers. Whatever subconscious thoughts they have begin to manifest within the environment. The more stressed the individual, the more frightening the manifestations become.*

727. *Only one survivor is left after a spaceship crashes on a lonely, desolate alien planet. There's no food, no water, and seemingly no way to get home. But this survivor is determined to get back to Earth.*

728. *The last of Earth's resources have been depleted and there is no choice but to colonize Mars. However, there isn't enough room for everyone and the populace must decide who will stay and who will go.*

729. *Suppose the above scenario holds true, except Mars is owned by a multi-trillion dollar company. Thus, only the rich are able to afford this life-saving relocation. The lower classes aren't going to stay on Earth without a fight.*

730. *Humans have colonized a distant planet after sullying Earth's natural resources. Thousands of years into the future, the colonists decide to return to Earth. There, they find a new life form has evolved.*

731. *A "New Earth" is found and instantly colonized. It isn't long before the colonists realize it isn't as Earth-like as they once thought.*

732. *Using the above scenario, suppose these colonists realize this new planet is not only too far from Earth to hold sustainable life, but old Earth has also been destroyed.*

733. *The entire galaxy has been searched for another planet that can sustain life. Not one is found. So, scientists decide to create a fabricated world to replace the old one.*

734. *In order to deal with an overwhelming Earth population, humans colonize space shuttles, then the moon, then distance planets. Eventually, the cosmos itself evolves to get rid of the parasitic invaders.*

735. *The first colonists on a lonely, distant planet are bored out of their minds with the limited activities available to them. As a result, they invent a new game to take some of the edge off.*

736. *Imagine the above scenario, but rather than simply inventing a new game, the colonists decide they no longer want to stay on the planet. They want to go back to Earth. The only problem? There is no more Earth.*

737. Life on the new planet is going seemingly well until the first drop of rain falls. Unlike the water that drops on Earth, this liquid is akin to acid.

738. The planet a group of colonists land on is beautiful and seemingly perfect in every way. Then the gathered group realizes the planet's dark secret—it's alive.

739. To deal with overpopulation, colonists begin to inhabit the moon. Before long, they over colonize the rocky locale and knock it out of orbit.

740. Future humans do not colonize other planets, but rather space itself. They erect space stations that can be reached via giant plastic tubes.

741. A new planet is discovered that is able to support life. Humans want to colonize it, but they first must get past the giant tentacles protruding from the living planet.

742. Space stations are set up all over the universe. They are typically used for research purposes only, but then a hotel is erected in the middle of the cosmos.

743. The first colonists are sent out into space to inhabit a planet millions of miles away. They are placed into a deep sleep, but something goes horribly wrong. When they awake, they have no idea who they are or what their mission is.

744. Use the above scenario, but rather than focusing on the colonists working together to figure out who they are in an introspective tale, instead craft an external problem. Perhaps something nefarious on board doubles the problem? Or perhaps one of the colonists is the culprit for

the mistake, and they are the only one who can remember who they are?

745. Every planet in the universe has finally been colonized, but there are still humans without a home. As a result, research begins in hopes the next stop will be the sun.

746. There are a great deal of kinks that arise when humans first colonize another planet. Namely, overextension of gravity causes everyone to be glued to the floor.

747. In order to deal with Earth's overpopulation, a group of colonists are sent to another planet. However, when they get there they find out there is no room. They go to a new planet and find there is no space there either. They continue on their journey, desperate to find a home.

748. Imagine the above scenario, but suppose the colonists are let in with ease. Curiously, they do not see a previous group they knew were coming in before them. That's when the planet's dark secret is realized. It is not meant to support life, but rather get rid of Earth's excess population.

749. Colonists have been living on the planet for several hundred years now. The planet has been studied thoroughly, but there is a problem. Despite initial research, scientists failed to realize every thousand years a cataclysmic disaster occurs in the planet, and the colonists will be the first ones to find out.

750. The first group of colonists have now bestowed three generations on the new planet. Upon first arriving, they followed strict Earth rules and lived that way for several

decades. However, the youngest generation believes it's time for new rules to be adopted.

751. *A strange fever breaks out across the first planetary colony and no one quite knows what to make of it. It isn't like any kind of disease seen on Earth. Before long, everyone on the colony is inflicted with no cure in sight.*

752. *Use the above scenario, but suppose only a handful of colonists become very, very sick. You can use a "zombie-like" troupe and make them hyper aggressive, or create some other kind of sickness. Either way, the healthy colonists must now decide what to do with them.*

753. *Specialized police roam the galaxy to dole out tickets to colonists breaking space laws while travelling from planet-to-planet. Craft a narrative in which one such officer gets a shocking surprise when they investigate a ship that has been stalled in one of the more remote locations in the cosmos.*

754. *Humans have colonized a planet to the point of overpopulation. Now underground bio domes must be built. After breaking soil for the first time, the terrain begins to crumble. As it turns out, the planet is hollow inside.*

755. *Many refer to it as the "Incident on planet 409". As one can guess, it is the 409th planet that has been occupied by Earthlings. While the other colonization projects have gone off without a hitch, this one was a disaster. Every member that set up camp on the planet died without warning. Just what exactly happened on planet 409?*

756.   A planet that is 99.9% like Earth has been discovered by a group that wants to migrate to a new world. Despite the fact others know of its existence, and other colonies have been set up on less inhabitable planets, no one has taken this gorgeous planet. The group wonders why, but are only met with a "you don't want to go there" response. In spite of everything they know, or the lack thereof, they decide to begin colonization at once. Then...they find out why.

757.   A lot of things can happen when one is exploring space. There are so many aspects we don't know. For one unnamed character, they are about to experience all of them. Craft a story in which this character is in search of something, or perhaps someone, and their trip takes them from one end of the universe to the other; from childhood all the way to old age.

758.   A spaceship comes across the strangest thing imaginable. At first, the group on board thinks it is a small planet, but the readings show it is an organic substance. In spite of this, there are no real nuances to the form other than it's circular in nature. Then, without warning, the eye they are looking at opens.

759.   Overpopulation has forced humans to colonize more than just the planets, but also the stars themselves. This creates a huge fraction between those that have their home on planets and those that have their home on Earth. When tensions are at there highest, both sets of humans find a

new threat. There's no more room on either stars or planets.

760. *The Earth goes through many different cycles of extinction. Current predictions dictate humankind is undergoing another mass extinction event, the 6th pr "Holocene extinction". Not only has a great number of animals become extinct in recent years, but fears are both humans and animals will be wiped from the face of the planet within the next fifty years. Imagine that, in order to escape this fate, humans begin to colonize the moon. However, when the humans' time is up, is there really escaping the inevitable?*

761. *The humans don't colonize other planets due to overpopulation, or their thirst for knowledge, or to drain natural resources. No, the humans of the future have become completely at one with their natural environment and only wish to colonize for one purpose: To bask in the beauty of a new world.*

762. *A real estate mogul owns several planets and builds luxury hotels and homes on each one. It isn't long before the costs of manning these buildings becomes much higher than the end profit. As a result, they decide to hire a team of mercenaries to blow up all of the planets in order to recoup the insurance money.*

763. *A small group of humans are the first colonists on Mars. For many years, they live in tiny biodomes funded from a crowdsourcing campaign. When developers want to move*

in, claiming they "bought" the planet from the government, the group refuses to go down without a fight.

764. *After Earth is destroyed, there are two colonies that exist on Mars. One group lives on the surface level, toiling day in and day out to make the planet hospitable for human life. The other group is the filthy rich, living on elaborate free-floating stations orbiting the planet. They are waiting to get the word they can migrate to the planet. However, frustrated with how the rich are essentially causing them to die slaving away on the red planet, the lower classes begin to think of a plot to destroy the wealthy.*

765. *An unnamed character is sent to inspect the colonists to ensure everything is adhering to governmental regulations. Once their ships docks, however, they find out there is no one on the planet at all. That's when the real trouble begins.*

766. *After Earth is no longer inhabitable, other planets are soon colonized. After millions of years of living on these other planets, a group of explorers return to the original blue planet and find it is able to support life once more. Draft a narrative that deals with these new Earth colonists.*

Military

As idealistic as space exploration sounds, it is not going to be all sunshine and roses. The history of the human race has been tainted with wars for centuries, be it because of greed, a need of resources, or simply a face that launched a thousand ships. If mankind is able to travel to the stars, there's no question warfare will follow.

767. *While exploring the farthest reaches of space, a lone astronaut witnesses a catastrophic event on another planet. Thinking themselves merely unlucky, the unnamed character doesn't know the planet is actually inhabited and it wasn't a random event that occurred, but the beginning stages of war.*

768. *As an ambassador from Earth, an unnamed character's job is to merely live on this strange world and answer questions regarding culture, biology, and so forth. It's an easy enough gig and this planet's inhabitants are even starting to grow on them. That is, until the unnamed character accidentally overhears a conversation surrounding two military leaders. As it turns out, they've been gathering intel for an upcoming attack.*

769. *An astronaut sits on the ledge of a space shuttle, watching the Earth from a lonely distance. They are counting down the days until their research stint is over when a passing spacecraft breaks their train of thought. It's followed by another craft, then another. It isn't long before a series of bombs falls right in front of their eyes. As the clouds of dust and debris clear, they ponder if they are the last human alive.*

770. *Humans are now a multi-planet species, having colonized distant worlds. Everything is seemingly going well until one planet launches a surprise attack on another.*

771.   On more of a micro scale, envision colonists have finally lived free from Earth's resources for several years. Before long, the colony declares their independence. Earth is quick to respond with an iron thumb.

772.   An unnamed character has been thrust into an intergalactic war despite being so young. Recruits are hard to come by, so the government is forced to draft any capable soldier. To protect them from the fight, the character's relative gives them a talisman, which they subsequently lose on the way to the battlefield.

773.   In order to gain an upper advantage against their enemies, members of a planet craft large iron giants. The goal is to release these robotic monoliths onto the planet and then allow them to win the war. However, there is a glitch in the system and the robots begin to attack well before they make it to the other planet.

774.   An unnamed character is in charge of leading an all out military attack against an invading planet. They are going over tactics with their most trusted advisor. Later, they discover the advisor is secretly working for the other side.

775.   In a very common military tactic, inhabitants of a planet cut off all food supply to another, essentially working to starve their enemies. The tactic is especially useful because this planet is devoid of its own natural resources.

776.   To cut their enemies down to size, one group of space denizens begin to send their sick to the offending planet.

The plan backfires when they discover members of that planet are immune to the disease.

777. When an intergalactic treaty is broken, it culminates in the first multi-planet war. The only problem? It was all just a simple misunderstanding.

778. At the Intergalactic Peace Summit, representatives of hundreds of planets make negotiations regarding new territory. Things seem to go well until one representative commits a major slight against another, prompting war.

779. Overpopulation and lack of resources has caused many of Earth's inhabitants to settle on a distant planet. Those who remain will likely live out their short lives on a wounded Earth. But that's not what happens. Those left behind fix the problems and a few thousand years later, they show up on the distant planet, declaring war.

780. War is over and an unnamed character sets upon a ravaged planet to collect someone dear to them. They have no way of knowing whether they are alive or dead until they are found.

781. An unnamed character enters into a planetary war not for honor or valor, but to protect the one(s) they love.

782. A weak unnamed character knows they will probably be one of the first ones killed in battle. That is, until they discover a device that will completely change their fate, as well as the outcome of the war.

783.   A member of the military is being held ransom by the enemy. In order for their release to happen, half of the planet's resources are demanded.

784.   A huge missile is aimed at an enemy planet, who is then threatened with war if certain demands aren't met. Unfortunately, no one realizes there is a kink in the launch system, so if the missile is fired, it will blow up without affecting the enemy planet at all.

785.   After a few minor invasions, Earth launches a series of attacks on an alien planet. The problem is not enough research has been done on the enemy. Thus, when a series of Earthlings arrive to begin an on-the-ground assault, it's quickly learned their enemy is not corporeal.

786.   Earthlings have arrived on the planet with one mission: seize the kingdom and take control. However, the invaders did not realize the members of this planet would be so good at guerrilla warfare.

787.   Imagine the above scenario, but rather than the members of this planet outright attacking Earthlings, the planet is completely vacant. Earthlings believe they've won...until they return to their ships and find they have all been blown up.

788.   In a similar scenario, human invaders find their enemies already dead on the battlefield. They are confused, but relieved they do not have to fight after all. As they are getting rid of the shells of their enemies, one human realizes the "bodies" are actually just a type of advanced suit.

789. *In the future, humans can fight space wide wars from the comfort of their chairs. The same cannot be said for their enemies.*

790. *The best way to combat an enemy force is to go after their resources. This is the mindset Earthlings take as they invade a Martian camp. They destroy all resources only to later discover they were the very things they needed after the war is over.*

791. *Planets of equal measure and might begin to attack each other. After countless lives are lost and resources are depleted, a truce is declared. In order to show solidarity, an interplanetary ball is thrown. Everyone is invited. However, not everyone is on board with this truce and they plan to use this event to showcase their dissent.*

792. *After a long and particularly grueling battle, the rulers of two planets decide to cut down on the bloodshed by fighting to the death themselves. The winner will enslave the people of the other.*

793. *Although many science fiction scenarios depict a planet being invaded by small units, chances are if humans were to invade a distant planet, it would be on a very large-scale. In this scenario, craft a narrative in which humans have dropped an atomic bomb on another planet and species.*

794. *The last non-inhabited planet is found. Instantly, a number of different groups begin to target the planet, hoping their victory will allow them to stake claim to the region.*

795. *Warfare across space has been raging for many centuries. One day it simply stops. The populace of each planet has become so accustomed to hatred, they do not know what to do now that peace is at hand.*

796. *All out planetary war has cost the lives of many and there seems to be no stopping. That's when the citizens of each planet decides to take up arms against those in charge of declaring war in the first place.*

797. *A group of mercenaries are the most powerful killing force on the planet. They have liberated countless planets and wreaked havoc on others. They are essentially unstoppable, but they are also very expensive.*

798. *The next great civil war is now underway, but it isn't limited to Earth. In fact, the civil war is between Mars and Earth, and the red planet is fighting to break free and form its own government system.*

799. *An unnamed character stows away on a vessel headed to another planet. Their only goal is to escape sentencing for a couple of petty crimes they've committed. What they don't realize, however, is they are on board a military craft that is headed into the heart of war.*

800. *An alliance is broken when an heir to the royal throne is kidnapped, triggering an interplanetary war. The King of Mars is threatening to destroy another planet if their progeny is not returned home safely. Too bad it's the heir behind the whole thing, using this as a ruse to usurp the throne much quicker.*

801.   A war has been going on for several decades and it doesn't seem like it will ever end. On top of this, a plague has hit one of the outer planets hard—one not even involved in the war. Then, a new, but rudimentary biological weapon is developed. One planet involved in the war begins to mine these plague victims, sending them to their enemy.

802.   Wars fought in space do not look like they do in typical science fiction fashion. Rather than aerial dogfights and intergalactic spaceships, a new type of guerrilla warfare is utilized. "Military astronauts" wear specialized suits complete with powerful guns. Groups directly fight one another as they try to bombard their way onto the enemy planet.

803.   A grizzled war veteran recounts their days in the war to a group of children. It is a detailed and compelling piece. When the story is over, the sirens go off.

804.   The ruling class lives in one large space station that is the size of a small country. The planets in space are in their control, including the people within them who mine for resources. It isn't long before the fire of rebellion catches.

805.   For thousands of years, there has not been a single war. In fact, the very concept of war has been lost for humanity. One day a dictator rises from the cosmos and reintroduces the meaning to the universes' populations.

Time Travel

I don't know about you, but even if I was unable to outright change history, I would still want a chance to see it. Can you imagine witnessing the fall of Rome firsthand? Or peering over Einstein's shoulder when he came up with his theory of relativity? It's the stuff we dream of because we so desperately want to become a part of history ourselves. Perhaps it is through that theory that time travel may one day be possible, whether on a micro or macro level.

806.   *Thanks to Einstein, one of the theories about space travel is it will rely on the theory of relativity. Therefore, the faster one travels through space, the slower they will go through time. Now, imagine it has been projected a high speed of space travel will allow one to visit the past in a specialized spacecraft. The mission ends up being a failure. When the astronaut returns home, not only do they have no tales to speak of, but they arrive 40 years in the Earth's future.*

807.   *An unnamed character invents a time machine, but because of their limited knowledge of science and its overall lack of power, it only goes ten minutes into the past.*

808.   *A 30 year old writer discovers a time machine and goes back in time, hoping to capitalize on all of the stories they've written at an earlier age. The problem? Public tastes change over time. For variations, the character can be any kind of creative.*

809.   *"The butterfly effect" is the idea that even a small, seemingly insignificant change can have dire consequences when it comes to time travel. In this scenario, create a story*

in which a subtle change creates a domino effect and leads to a cataclysmic event.

810. An unnamed character continues to go back in time to stop their loved one from dying. No matter how many times they go back, their loved meets the same unfortunate fate, only in different ways. Eventually, the character must learn to let go.

811. An unnamed character is found wandering the streets of a heavily populated city. A local law enforcement officer speaks with them at length, fearing something might be wrong. The character claims to be from a time and place too far in the future to be believable. At least, until the character shows proof.

812. Suppose the above holds true, but rather than from external viewpoints dealing with the time traveller, the story focuses on the traveller themselves. Additionally, the traveller is sent back in time, but loses all memories once they get there.

813. An unnamed character goes back in time for the sole purpose of stopping their favorite band from breaking up. Rather than fulfilling their goal, the character inadvertently causes a new rift, which results in them ousting a member and taking over.

814. A group of time travellers are sent on a government mission to stop a nefarious regime leader from stepping into power. Although they successfully complete their mission, a new, more powerful force ends up taking over.

815. *Imagine the above scenario, but only one secret agent is sent back in time. They too end up stopping the cruel tyrant, but then become one as a result.*

816. *An unnamed character is sent back in time to stop a person from becoming evil later in life. After warning the child of their dire future, the youth becomes evil at a much earlier age.*

817. *Without warning, a school bus is thrown off course and lands in a ditch. The shaken students step off the bus and find themselves in a different time.*

818. *While arguing in a time machine, two unnamed characters accidently set their course off track—by a lot. Although they meant to go a few hundred years into the future, they accidently go two million years into the past.*

819. *A scientist believes they have perfected time travel and decide to use themselves as the first test subject. They want to take things slow, so they only go 20 years into the past. Everything works—sort of. Rather than sending themselves into the past, the scientist sends their conscious into the mind of their younger self.*

820. *Imagine the above scenario, but rather than sending themselves into the past, they send their younger self into the future.*

821. *An unnamed character goes into the past, intending to be a casual observer. They make strides to only witness history, not change it. Unbeknownst to them, they end up in famous*

paintings and historic photographs. When they return to
their own time, they find they've become an urban legend.

822. *An unnamed character is curious to know what the future*
will hold for their hamlet. They use a time machine to jump
a century into the future, not realizing their little town will
be submerged by then.

823. *An unnamed character goes back in time to prevent the*
death of their favorite celebrity. Not only do they fail, but
they are accused of having a hand in it.

824. *While using an illicit substance, a character swears they*
have time jumped into another time period. Due to their
habitual drug use, no one believes them until they reach
into their pocket and find a series of photographs.

825. *To prove their experiences, a time traveller steals an object*
from the future before going back to their own time. They
gather everyone around to see the interesting piece of
technology, not realizing one important fact—it's a weapon
of mass destruction.

826. *In an attempt to change the course of victory, a nation*
sends a number of soldiers back in time to figure out the
enemy's exact location. What they don't know is that
enemy soldiers are in the process of doing the exact same
thing.

827. *An unnamed character attempts to visit different moments*
in their own timeline. Instead, they end up bringing back
different versions of themselves.

828. *After a bad storm, a body that succumbed to the elements is discovered. Curiously, the individual is wearing garb from a couple of centuries before. Furthermore, they look similar to someone who supposedly went missing during that time period.*

829. *As it turns out, one simply cannot time travel. However, in the future a device is invented that will allow one to see both past and future events.*

830. *While browsing the internet one day, an unnamed character gets an email notification. They think nothing of it until they realize it's been sent by their future self.*

831. *One day an unlucky individual begins to see a slew of good fortune. It starts with a lottery hit, then good stock investments, and so on, until they are the richest person on Earth. Everyone wants to know the big secret. Eventually the ruse is up. They are from the future and have been using what they know to make better decisions in the past.*

832. *An unnamed character experiences a case of unrequited love. In order to win their love's affections, they go back in time to orchestrate events to bring them together. It backfires with grave consequences. For a variation, perhaps the character does win their love's affection, but they realize their "love" wasn't really who they thought they were.*

833. *A time traveller goes into the past to witness a key historical event. While there, they are accidentally caught using a futuristic device and are instantly accused of practicing witchcraft.*

834.   *In the aforementioned scenario, suppose instead those that witness the odd display of the time traveller are in awe. The time traveller then amasses a large following and, eventually, creates their own religion.*

835.   *To prevent a large-scale cataclysmic event—which would eventually be humankind's downfall—a group of time travellers go into the past to prevent it from happening. As it turns out, that is exactly what sets off the event in the first place.*

836.   *While cleaning their grandparent's basement, an unnamed character stumbles across a strange looking box. They can't quite resist touching the odd object. As they do, they are suddenly transported into the same house. When they see their grandparent again, they are a child.*

837.   *After years of tinkering, an unnamed character has finally invented a time machine. No, they don't want to change the mind of an unrequited love or stop someone from dying. What they want is to simply take over the world.*

838.   *An unnamed character suddenly hears a familiar voice on their old transistor radio. The voice states they are from the future. The character believes them because many events come to pass. What they don't realize, however, is the voice belongs to their future self. For a variation, the voice can belong to a friend, family member, or someone else they might recognize.*

Alternative Universe

The idea of creating a world completely different than the one we know factors into many genres. In fact, the very backbone of fiction writing is the ability to craft your own world. However, these imaginary places are especially common in science fiction. Since sci-fi deals largely with observation, exploration, and the *why* of things, one common motif is rediscovering our humanity through an entirely different universe.

839. *One of the greatest joys of being human is falling in love. What if this universe had no love at all? There is motivation and desire, but no love. Suppose an unnamed character experiences it for the first time.*

840. *Suppose there is another planet hidden behind the sun, within the same distance as ours. Further still, suppose this planet evolved in the same way, but with one noticeable difference. Instead of humans becoming the dominate species, another one does.*

841. *A crew of ragtag space explorers discover a wormhole. Being the curious bunch they are, they throw caution to the wind and go through it. There, they meet another ragtag bunch, warning them about going through the wormhole.*

842. *Suppose the ragtag bunch only finds an entrance to another wormhole behind the one they've just stepped through. They decide to step through this one as well, only to find yet another wormhole. They go on and on until they realize they've stepped inside a giant maze in the cosmos.*

843. *An unnamed character discovers a portal underneath their bed. Inside, they are taken to an alternate reality with one small difference: there are no humans.*

844. *A young child discovers there is a moveable portal inside the house. It can be used to go just about anywhere. Being as young as they are, the child usually uses the portal to sneak snacks from the kitchen or candy from the store down the street. One day they enter the portal and find a different world entirely.*

845. *In an alternate reality, an individual's screen name is more than just a name picked out for themselves. It's a direct representation of who they are. From being a canine deity as wolfgod24, to a young visitor from another world as starchild.*

846. *Suppose every religion on Earth is correct. Plus, not only are they real, but depending on the different location in the world, one might see acts from different deities, gods, and goddesses. Additionally, every once in a while, they choose to compete against each other to earn the most human belief.*

847. *Taking a page from "Buffy the Vampire Slayer", suppose on every Halloween the populace has the ability to transform into their costumes for just one night.*

848. *Suppose a minor miscalculation in the history of the Earth caused evolution to occur, but with one key difference: There is no intelligent life to speak of.*

849. *In this scenario, picture a scenario in which humankind does not live on the Earth, but rather they are creatures of the sea.*

850. *A portal to another world is opened inside an unnamed character's living room. From inside a glorious creature or frightening entity, out steps hundreds of different copies of the character.*

851. *An astronaut discovers a wormhole which leads to an alternate reality. Having just lost the one they love, they are hopeful they will find them alive in this reality.*

852. *Suppose the above scenario holds true and after searching for their loved one, the astronaut discovers they are gone in this new reality too. They then search for another wormhole and another new reality—then another and another, hoping they will find a world where their love does not perish.*

853. *Envision a world where humans are not the only animals that have evolved towards intelligent life. Instead, a number of animals have evolved to have cultures, societies, clothing, speech, and so on. For a variation, remove humans from the equation.*

854. *In the Holographic Universe theory, the running idea is that the world we know is more or less a hologram of something else. Take this idea and expand upon it. Suppose the world is a hologram and is being projected by the "real" world. What is that world like? What about the beings that*

live there? More importantly, why create a hologram like
our world in the first place?

855. *A collection of connected alternate universes is called a*
"multiverse". Imagine an unnamed character has just
stumbled into a universe that is a stepping stone to get into
any parallel universe imaginable. Whoever controls this
one portal controls all of the worlds.

856. *Envision an alternate universe in which the law of gravity*
no longer applies. Imagine how Earth life would develop if
there was no way to ground anything at all.

857. *On the reverse end of the spectrum, envision a universe in*
which Earth's gravity holds far more weight. Even just a
fraction more intensity can reshape the way creatures
adapt to stronger gravity.

858. *In this scenario, there is a parallel universe known as the*
"dual world". In it, opposite events and behavior occur. For
instance, if an individual was murderous and unkind in
our reality, then in this duel world they would be saintly
and benevolent. Without knowing this information, an
unnamed character gets trapped in this world and has no
idea who to trust.

859. *While exploring the basement of a local library, a group of*
teens discover an alternate dimension in which books are
reality and the "real" world aligns with the pages of books.

860. *In this dimension, humans are akin to Gods and at a*
certain age they are given their own planet to rule over. An
unnamed character happens across this dimension and is

instantly put into the rites of passage as they are the same,
or above, this special age.

861. A teen discovers a portal inside of their bedroom, but rather
than leading them anywhere extraordinary, the portal
leads to different points in the house.

862. An unnamed character discovers a portal that mirrors our
reality, except technology has been advanced hundreds of
years in the future.

863. Imagine the exact same scenario, but rather than
technology being from the future, suppose it is archaic—
centuries old.

864. A parallel universe is discovered to have 21st century
technology similar to our own. However, the culture is
extremely outdated. For instance, one could be accused of
witchcraft over the internet, or watch gladiators fight to the
death on reality TV.

865. The fabric of space and time suddenly begins to crumble,
allowing wormholes to appear all over the city. Rather than
stepping through them to see what interesting things they
might contain, the interesting "things" begin to step out.

866. An unnamed character is in the middle of filing for
bankruptcy after a business failure. In the process, they
stumble across a wormhole. In this world, they can retrieve
all kinds of fanciful objects, which they immediately sell.
The business begins to flourish, but it isn't long before
problems arise. For a unique variation, the individual can
sell exotic plants, pets, etc.

867. *While hiking through the woods, an unnamed character spots a glowing lake. From it, a small being steps out from another dimension. It isn't long before the government quarantines the section off, watching as creatures emerge one by one, each more grotesque than the last. For a variation, the creatures can go from smaller to bigger, passive to more aggressive, etc.*

868. *A child discovers a shadow universe underneath their bed. Rather than turning up anything frightening, the child only finds boring things like untapped energy sources, precious metals, and other resources.*

869. *The law of conservation of energy states that energy can neither be created nor destroyed, only transferred. As such, after suffering an unfortunate loss, an unnamed character finds a wormhole inside a graveyard that shows the new form their loved one has taken.*

870. *While walking home from school one day, an unnamed character finds someone who looks exactly like them. It's a strange sight since they are an only child. They decide to follow the odd doppelganger and are led to an entirely different reality.*

871. *A hapless hunter falls into their own trap: a wide hole covered with leaves. They expect to be pierced with dozens of spikes at the bottom, but instead find themselves falling from the sky into an alternate universe—one where animals hunt humans.*

Steampunk, Dieselpunk, & More

One prevalent subgenre of science fiction we previously touched upon is cyberpunk. While in this guide the focus is on cyber crime and security threats, in the actual genre the common theme is technology and what might happen if it was placed in a different time period. From that, the "punk" subgenres were born. In a nutshell there are four common classifications: steampunk, dieselpunk, decopunk, and atompunk. In all of these elements, the primary question is how would specific time periods change if given newer technology? For example, steampunk deals predominately with 19th century Victorian culture that utilizes steam power. Dieselpunk shoves current technology between World War I and II, while Decopunk reshapes the art culture in the 1920s to 1950s with modern technology. Finally, atompunk deals with the 1940s to 1960s, especially with the threat of atom bombs. If this was a lot to handle, keep in mind there are even more "punk" genre derivatives than the ones named, many of which we will touch upon.

872.   *There is a kingdom that runs purely on steampunk technology. When an upcoming invasion occurs, it's apparent the attackers have a clear advantage. An unnamed character invents something that will shape the entire course of the war.*

873.   Troubled by a long lost love, an inventor tinkers inside his
        quaint town home, attempting to create the loved one he
        lost so long ago.

874.   During a grand gala, a group of socialites are sweeping
        across the dance floor. With a deep rumble, the floor begins
        to rotate and lift up to the night sky. It's almost as if the
        group is waiting for something.

875.   An unnamed character invents a flying machine that looks
        like a giant bird with a basket underneath. To prove how
        masterful this creation is, the inventor invites a group of
        friends to enter this strange bird and fly across the world.

876.   A group of young schoolchildren decide to sneak past the
        headmaster and escape to the school's dank basement.
        There, they hear a strange clinking noise and follow it to a
        mad scientist. Lying on his work table is an automaton
        with deadly glowing eyes.

877.   A priest is disenfranchised when church attendance lowers
        and then stops altogether. As a result, they set about
        crafting an automaton based off the biblical notion of the
        devil in order to draw "sinners" into the light.

878.   A carriage is invented that does not require the use of
        horses. This "self-steering buggy" is an instant hit…until it
        starts to carry off its passengers to unknown destinations.

879.   To prevent an arranged marriage that is unwanted, an
        inventor crafts an automaton that is meant to look exactly
        like them. Naturally, this comes with unintended
        consequences.

880. *They came from the sky—the whole lot of them—in their steam powered flying balloons. They were a new type of pirate, and they were far deadlier than anyone could have imagined.*

881. *The World's Fair is drawing many inventors from around the country. Some are building new flying machines, while others are creating clockwork people. An unnamed character sits in the corner, crafting what will become a world-threatening weapon.*

882. *A young unnamed character loses their hand in a war. Fortunately, an inventor makes them a new one out of clockwork. Unfortunately, the hand seems to take on a life of its own.*

883. *The Great Depression never happened. As such, the Jazz era never really ended, and all that glitz and glam caused the country to make huge strides with technology.*

884. *Perhaps The Great Depression not only happened, but it was elongated. Now the country is on the verge of crumbling. Thankfully, a new invention takes hold that is set to change history and save millions.*

885. *Just after World War II begins, a new noxious gas is released upon many cities. As a result, many have taken to wearing strange gas masks that seem more robotic than rubber.*

886. *A ragtag team of hired mercenaries have been contracted by the government to break into a secret German bunker. What is notable about this group isn't the inventive*

weapons they use—far advanced for the era—but the fact they might not be entirely human.

887. Television has quickly replaced radio as the primary source of entertainment in most homes. Rather than going down without a fight, a sly broadcaster begins to send mind control waves to encourage the populace to steer clear of the "idiot box".

888. At the height of World War II, the Allied military powers are failing. Then, on the European landscape, the enemy soldiers see them—a large fleet of strange round planes reflecting the sun from a mirrored, chrome-like surface.

889. "The Future is Now" is one of the signs at the local inventor's fair. Everything is represented here—phones with videos displayed, flying cars, awesome ray guns. For the most part, everything is just for show, but one unnamed character is going to change all of that. They have invented something that not only works, but is going to take the world by storm—literally!

890. Deep within the mad scientist's lair, an unnamed character is trapped. Under a lone swinging bulb, this hero must find a way to escape before they are experimented on like all of the other wayward hippies ripped from the concert.

891. The great Space Race is on! But instead of landing on the moon, the United States aims a little too far and sends a group of astronauts to Mars.

892.   The Great War ends with total annihilation, but the people are resilient. They must live in this world with only moxie and ray guns as a means of survival.

893.   New machines for the kitchen have become all the rage, and all of the dainty housewives of the era are clamouring to get their own. That is, until these machines suddenly begin to react aggressively against their owners. Rather than letting someone else take care of these mechanical beings, these ladies take matters into their own hands.

894.   A private investigator is sent to determine why a bunch of hapless children are missing from an affluent suburban neighborhood. Things like this just don't happen in the '50s. The P.I. discovers these kids aren't vanishing by some horrible madman, but by culprits from out of this world.

895.   Sirens begin to blare all across the city. Against the ear-splitting shrill of the warnings, a group hurries into a fallout shelter that has been crafted underground. Sealed up tight, the first bomb goes off. That's when one individual notices a strange shadow emerging from the other end of the tunnel.

896.   An unnamed character excitedly receives their allowance from their loving parents. Time to take a trip to the picture show! Excitedly, they gather up their friends and make their way to the theatre. After putting on the 3D glasses, they take their seats. Soon, they realize the picture isn't 3D. It's 4D.

897.   The youth of the 60s era seem to be obsessed with rock and roll. The older generation believes it's completely sullying their values. In order to manage these "wild" teens, parents buy special products that restrain these rock and roll urges—through mind control.

898.   On a remote island, early in the history of humans, a small tribe is busy harnessing electricity to outdo their rock-using neighbors.

899.   In ancient Greece, an inventor suddenly wakes from a strange dream in which they flew. Determined to make their dream a reality, they start working on the very first flying machine.

900.   While gathered around a campfire, a group of tribesmen tell stories of days past. One of them begins speaking of "blue monsters" that will bring about the end of the stone age. The others deem this person mad...until the robots show up.

901.   The plague doctors were a group of medical practitioners that arose during the Middle Ages. Many of them were simply farmers tasked with removing the dead and helping the diseased in any way possible. Craft a world in which these doctors are far more than meets the eye, using advanced technology to help the inflicted.

902.   An elderly scholar pours over an ancient manuscript deep within the caverns of an old castle. Their gnarled finger runs across the notes, over and over again. At last, eureka! They have found a way to harness the sun.

903. *Many are accused of nefarious, evil practices during the Middle Ages. Some of those who have been rounded up and put into cages aren't actual cohorts of the devil. Instead, they are inventors, harnessing advanced technologies.*

Superheroes, Transhumanism, & Mighty Beings

The concept of "mighty beings" has been around for centuries. Many Greek figures, for example, focus on human figures that have been blessed in some extraordinary way. Theseus destroyed the minotaur, Odysseus went on a perilous journey that lasted ten years, and Hercules was born to slay any monster that came into his path. The term "superhero" itself is from the early 1900s. Since then, masked crusaders have become a staple in pop culture. The idea we can be something more than what we are hasn't left our subconscious. Focus on that when crafting your tale. Do not stop at the idea these humans have been imbued with amazing gifts. Give them additional reasons for being. Make them real enough to cast shadows. Above all else, remember their special characteristics should be secondary to who they are as people. In doing so, you will not only make a tale that is incredible, but also believable.

Superpowers

If you could have any superpower, what would it be? Some might opt for invisibility, hoping they might be able to rob a bank or spy on a cheating lover. Others might want to have super strength, able to punch bad guys into the atmosphere. Still, there might be more unusual powers, such as the ability to transform any loaf of bread into a pile of money, or herald dominion over all rodents. The kind of superpowers that may be granted in science fiction are as varied as your imagination.

904. *Everyone is special. At least they are in this world. Everyone has been born with a power. The problem? No one knows what it is until they get older, usually when they need their power the most.*

905. *An unnamed character is on a blind date with someone they are attracted to. Things go better than expected. Later, while at their date's home, they ask where the bathroom is. The directions are rather hazy and, inadvertently, the unnamed character stumbles across their date's secret lair.*

906. *A mad scientist creates a serum that is set to turn them into a super villain. Eagerly, they go to drink it, only to discover they've accidentally switched out the formula with their child's bottle.*

907. *Craft a tale in which a disenfranchised superhero, so perturbed by their many defeats, decides to become a super villian. Rather than being stopped by another villain, it is their archenemy who helps them see the light.*

908. *While walking home from a comic book store, a teen is hit by a truck carrying a collection of toxic waste. Unfortunately, they die due to radiation poisoning. However, while at the morgue, a hapless attendant leaves the body with the window open during a lightning storm. After a stray bolt hits the body, a new, but bizarre hero emerges.*

909. *Imagine the above scenario, but oddly enough, radioactive waste really is the way to become a superhero. After being*

hit, the teenager takes on the same powers as the hero featured in the comic they are holding.

910. *An unnamed character is a member of a league of superheroes. Currently, there is an asteroid heading to Earth and everyone has a different opinion on how to deal with it. That's when things get heated (no pun intended).*

911. *Many are aware there are groups of individuals who are considered "real superheroes". They walk the streets of their cities, dressed in a costume of their own creation, and doing good while under the guise of their self-created moniker. They have no powers to speak of and are considered "real people". Except for one. One hero joins these normal individuals knowing it will make their true identity that much harder to believe if it is discovered.*

912. *After nuclear fallout, a strange group of super powered individuals emerge from the rubble. Some set about recreating the new world, while others seek to destroy it.*

913. *An unnamed character, frustrated with the state of the world, crafts a metal giant they can step into and fix it. The problem is, although they are rightfully a superhero, without their specialized suit, they are powerless.*

914. *An unnamed character cowers beneath the gaze of several assailants in an alleyway. The criminals demand that money or valuables be handed over. In a flash, a masked stranger crashes down and shoos the others away. The character rejoices too quickly. This isn't a superhero. It's a villain.*

915. *A superhero is extremely unique, far different than all of the others. Rather than having one superpower, they have many. However, their powers will change based upon their mood.*

916. *A new serum hits the streets, allowing just about anyone to become a superhero. Those with a lot of money have access to the serums with the best powers, while those who can only afford knockoff versions experience unusual side effects.*

917. *A superhero's only power is to manipulate human emotion. At first, they find this power to be useless. Then they realize just how valuable shaping someone else's feelings can be.*

918. *For a few decades now, a lone superhero has kept the world safe. Wayward meteors are knocked out of the way, and evil villains are stopped within minutes. Every kind of disaster has been stopped by this hero's hand. Then one day this beloved hero perishes from the worst enemy—old age. Craft a narrative in which the world must deal with their death. Who will save the populace now?*

919. *In a similar concept, craft a narrative in which a superhero must deal with the fact they are getting older and, before long, they must hang up the metaphorical cape.*

920. *In this world, a small percentage of the population has been born with innate gifts. However, the only way to release these powers is to find one's soul mate. Or, rather, their perfect sidekick.*

921. *A machine is invented that is supposed to unleash mankind's true potential. Instead, the machine creates superheroes. This works by drawing out the individual's best talent and then exaggerating it. Craft a narrative in which an unnamed character is entering this machine for the first time. For a more complex scenario, envision a character who has no talent at all.*

922. *There is a serum that can turn anyone into a superhero. However, in order to obtain these additional powers, the individual must be willing to lose one of their five senses.*

923. *Envision a scenario in which an unnamed character has powers and becomes one of the world's best superheroes. However, this does not come without a price. After they save a life, the rest of that individual's life is taken from the hero's. Thus, if someone is saved and gets to live ten more years, ten years is taken from the hero.*

924. *After years of entering one bad relationship after the other, a villain finally falls in love and contemplates hanging up their villainy for good. It isn't long, however, before they find out their beloved is actually their archenemy. For a variation, it can be a superhero that falls in love with a villain, two superheroes, etc.*

925. *In this world, there is only one superhero and they are extremely strong and talented, but...not very capable. In fact, they are something of a bumbling idiot.*

926. *Although superheroes are usually born with their powers, some develop them later in life. This unnamed character*

develops them a heck of a lot later. They believe the strange aches and pains they feel are a result of going through middle age. Then one day their full powers emerge.

927. After losing a bunch of victims to the enemy, a superhero decides they can no longer deal with the loss. They fly to a remote island and stay there. It's the job of one unnamed character to talk some sense into the caped crusader.

928. Superheroes are born in this world, but only a select few. An unnamed character should consider themselves lucky when they are born with powers. But they have the lamest powers on Earth. Still, when a new villain arises, and all of the other heroes are held captive or destroyed, they have to try and help, even if that means using their regrettable powers.

929. The power of this superhero is to change their appearance at will. They can essentially become anyone in the world. The problem is, the more identities they take on, the more they forget who they really are.

930. A group of teens are kidnapped by the government as part of a covert operation. The goal? To create real superheroes that could save the world from destruction. They are marginally successful.

931. An unnamed character's superpower is regeneration, allowing them to effectively become immortal. After hundreds of years, the character has finally become bored by life and sets out to save one last life.

932.   A collection of superheroes are trying to make a plan on how to avoid a disaster that would completely destroy the world. There is a lot of talk about how to go about saving humanity, but no one is making any headway. That is, until they finally realize the only way they can save humanity is if one of them commits the ultimate sacrifice.

933.   A superhero's power is the ability to retrieve someone else's memories. They've gotten quite good at it and can even do so remotely. The problem is, they can't get rid of the memories once they have them. For a variation of the prompt, play around with the idea of simply having too many memories/thoughts. Or perhaps no knowing which memory was theirs or someone else's.

934.   In a world of superheroes, an unnamed character feels left out. They feel like they have nothing to offer the world. Then one day they discover their power—to take away another's pain and replace it with something far greater.

935.   A superhero has become bored with the same routine. Save someone in the morning, someone else in the afternoon, and someone else in the evening. Go to bed. Repeat. Then they wake up one day and find they have no superpowers to speak of.

Human Enhancement

In many superhero mythos, humans are either born or they are made into a hero by some outer force. No matter what, some suspension of disbelief is required. This section deals with the technological side of human enhancement. Transhumism, body modification, and similar ideologies address the idea of redefining the human condition through self-fabricated means. In some cases, the goal is mere aesthetics, while in others it is to prolong and enhance life.

936.   *Amongst the bric-a-brac, in a lone junkyard, an unnamed character sits quietly while the night looms menacingly. Piece by piece, they fuse parts of the junk to various parts of their body. As the last piece is placed with a gentle whir, they know it's time.*

937.   *The newest smartphone is out and it's all of rage. It can do things many never even dreamed of. There's just one catch. In order for it to work properly, users must have it fused to their hands.*

938.   *In order to increase human intelligence, a small implant is placed just behind the ear, giving individual's the ability to download additional information as a type of external storage device. Generally, one has to manually upload information. However, it isn't long before the system begins to glitch and the user has no control over what gets uploaded to their brain.*

939.   *Imagine a different implant is designed to foster communication at a rapid pace. Rather than needing to use a computer to send a message or "Like" a page, the user is able to interact with social media and advanced communication merely through their thoughts. Craft a narrative in which an unnamed character uses the*

technology and becomes overwhelmed with the inability to have a moment to themselves.

940. Robotic limbs and organs are all of rage. But there is an unforeseen problem. In some of the cases, these limbs will lock up without warning. This is never talked about by manufacturers and it happens so rarely, it has not made its way into the media. Thus, it comes as quite a shock for an unnamed character who suddenly finds themselves planted to the ground.

941. New fabricated eyes allow blind patients to see, even if they have been blind since birth. It's a great feat and many commend modern medicine. But there is a problem. Installed in the eyes are a type of computer system that allows information to be processed to the brain. When this glitches, what people "see" becomes jumbled. Some even start to see out of eyes of others.

942. Envision the above scenario, but rather than seeing through someone else's eyes, these poor souls see random hallucinations. For some, these visions are joyful. For others, they are dark and scary.

943. A lone hacker has been using implants to advance their humanity for quite some time. They've replaced an eye that allows them to utilize night vision and heat scanning, and have also installed an implant in their arm that gives them access to the internet at all times. They have even modified their legs to give them the ability to sustain shock when jumping from a large height. Eventually, they replace

portions of their brain to boost intelligence and soon,
without realizing it, they begin to lose many human
emotions. Namely, empathy.

944. *Plastic surgery allows ugly people to become more*
beautiful, despite beauty being entirely subjective. One
unnamed character has been through several operations,
but this new one isn't merely aesthetic. They want to
become so perfect, they can easily be mistaken for a robot.
Then, they are.

945. *New contact lenses hit the market that allow one to access*
the internet with the blink of an eye—literally. While most
are happy with their new hands-free accessory, a small
fraction of users report a serious problem. They can't take it
off.

946. *At a remote research laboratory, a group of subjects are*
fitted with different technological components. Some are
given bionic limbs, while others reserve faux nerve endings.
Although kept secluded from each other, the group of
"patients" find a way to tunnel to each other and plan a full
blown revolt.

947. *An unnamed character is given new eyes after losing them*
in war. They are told they might come with a glitch known
as "telescope eyes" which increases vision range
dramatically and allows one to see objects at a far distance.
This occurs a few times before the character realizes they
can use this new "gift" to spy on the neighbors. Soon, they
become obsessed.

948. *New "changeable" contacts are all the rage. Simply by thinking, one can have green eyes, blue eyes, or even unique eyes like all black or cat-like. At first, the popular trend is fun. Then the technology begins to glitch, causing these new contacts to not only get stuck to the eyes, but stuck on a certain look. As a result, new prejudices based on eye type emerge.*

949. *A young kid is constantly in their room, tinkering with strange little mechanical objects they find here and there. What their parents don't know is they have been implanting these objects onto their own body, determined to become something more than human.*

950. *While researching osteoporosis and other bone diseases, scientists create a new exoskeleton that comes with a strange side effect—anti-gravity.*

951. *An unnamed character has been given metal-like implants inside an arm, hoping it will help set what is broken. They awake in the middle of the night with severe pain. Once it subsides they enter a heavy sleep. Upon waking, they find more of the strange substance has taken root. Before long, almost 45% of their body is covered with the odd metal growth.*

952. *The new generation has pushed transhumanism to new heights. Their forms have become so augmented, many no longer look human. Fearing they could easily overthrow the government, the older members of the population begin to round up the "changed".*

953. Only a small percentage of the population can afford artificial organs, implants, and other faux human components. As a result, it is not uncommon for individuals with these upgrades to be robbed by thieves who rip their new technological parts straight from their bodies.

954. A scientist begins to use his own body to test specific biological components and how they might successfully merge with technology. During one such experiment, the scientist replaces their blood with a synthetic substance. At first, everything seems to be going well. They feel, look, and act healthy. Then the scientist suddenly becomes violently ill. That's when things take a turn for the worst.

955. Technology might not only work to cause effects in humans. Imagine a scenario in which lab animals are fitted with technological devices to test how they might respond to humans, and it isn't before long these animals become hyper intelligent and revolt.

956. As part of transhumanist experimentation, a group of toddlers are known as "the children". They have all had some parts of themselves replaced with advanced technology. Scientists are only gauging whether or not a younger body is more susceptible to these augmentations. What they don't expect is for these young humans to develop a collective mind, and become fully detached from humanity and form their own life form.

957. The populace is quite happy with their new technological components. Individuals live longer and can perform

advanced feats. Many even claim they have better relationships. But if all is going so well, why is there a secret underground movement to remove these components?

958. *New skin implants have become all the rage. People are able to transform their skin color or allow moveable pictures to dance across their body. It isn't long before advertisers using the technology to allow individuals to become walking billboards. An unnamed character is so down on their luck, they rent out every inch of their skin.*

959. *Taking a page out of cyber crime, suppose technological components have become a popular trend for the future populace. They can replace limbs, enhance vision, and essentially improve their lot in life. Irritated by this new form of blind consumerism, a hacker begins to hijack this technology and the populace with it.*

960. *A young, lonely child has been fitted with a technological component after being diagnosed with a serious medical condition. The only plus side of their unfortunate circumstance is the new implant comes with communication technology. One day, while fiddling with it, the child taps into the implant of another child and the two form a bond.*

961. *A new cult emerges deep within the mountains. No, it isn't centered on a specific deity. These individuals are obsessed with enhancing their forms with technology. Many do not see them as a threat, but the government does.*

962.   New technological implants similar to gills emerge. It isn't before long a whole subset of humans decide to live deep within the ocean depths.

963.   Traditionalists claim there are only two distinct genders, while modernists claim there is more than one. The transhumanists of the future decide to physically create different subsets of gender. Before long, there are several new genders. Some within society are not so accepting of this new form of human.

964.   As a result of new transhumanists, a group of "technophobes" emerge. They see technologically advanced humans as a threat and have taken to rounding them up and inflicting all kinds of pain and brutality.

965.   An unnamed character has transformed more than 50% of their body using rudimentary machines and technological equipment they bought secondhand. While many who undertake this kind of feat are doing so to beat aging and death, this individual is doing so to win back their love.

966.   An individual has tattoos covering every inch of their body. This isn't for aesthetics or even some kind of meaning. No, each of their tattoos carries specific pockets of data, and they are willing to part with this sensitive information—for a price.

967.   An unnamed character wakes up in an unfamiliar hotel room after being attacked in an alleyway. They hear the sound of machinery nearby and look down. And scream.

Their bottom half has been replaced with strange metal components.

Other Changes

In the science fiction genre, the idea of change plays a significant role in many great works of literature. Kafka's *Metamorphosis* is a great example of how physical changes should only be a catalyst to the narrative and not overtake it. Changes should, by their inclusion, work to underline the main point or theme. What do these changes represent for the characters? For society? For humanity as a whole? Knowing these elements will give you a better understanding of how these changes can work to impact the world in some way, whether on the micro or macro level.

968. *One day an unnamed character wakes up and, with some confusion, notices everything looks larger than usual. They soon realize it's because they have regressed to their childhood body. Thankfully (or perhaps unfortunately), they still maintain their adult mentality. For a variation, consider the opposite. An individual wakes up elderly, but maintains their younger mindset.*

969. *A scientist and an astrologist are working together on a serum that can be used to mimic the traits of a certain astrological sign. After an accident at a lab, a hapless worker gets a full dose of what they are working on. Now, almost hourly, the poor individual's personality changes to match a new sign.*

970.   Envision the scenario above, but instead of merely taking on personality traits, the individual bears the physical appearances of these signs as well.

971.   A new company begins to offer "ChangeX" with the slogan "Become who you really are!". The technology is supposed to allow individuals to alter their appearances and bypass expensive plastic surgery. The only downside? The change only lasts for 24 hours.

972.   Consider the above scenario, but imagine a narrative in which an unnamed character abuses the nature of this system As a result, instead of crafting a unique avatar, they become someone else entirely.

973.   An unnamed character wakes up one day to find their whole family has been replaced by small, crawling bugs of all types. When they go outside, they are shocked to see it isn't just their dear family, but the whole world! For a variation, make it so everyone but the character has turned into an animal.

974.   An unnamed character wakes up one day to find they have turned into an animal (perhaps the type is a reflection of their personality). It's hard to get help from anyone, especially when animal control is the first thing called. Note: If the character has been transformed into a bug, they might go unnoticed.

975.   They call the criminal "The Body Snatcher". They are a rogue scientist who sells the corpses of the young to the old. Sometimes their method of a secretive surgery, by way of

kidnapping, works but more often than not, the elderly don't look young. They look mangled.

976. *Perhaps "The Body Snatcher" doesn't steal bodies at all—at least, not corpses. Instead, envision a scenario in which this criminal "jumps" inside the bodies of unsuspecting victims and fully controls them. Once he has used them to excess, he moves to his next victim.*

977. *After a night of binge drinking, an unnamed character wakes up with a massive headache. Everything seems slowed down. Then, out of the blue, things return normal. It isn't before long the individual realizes things don't "seem" slowed down—they are! And they're the cause of it.*

978. *An environmentalist is determined to save the trees. So much so, they chain themselves to a particularly huge redwood to prevent development over the land. The first day, they feel a little itchy, but ignore it. The second, they feel hot from the inside out. By the third, they begin to sprout leaves.*

979. *Most have seen the commercials featuring "the little blue pill" and what it might do for one's libido. Craft a scenario in which a man takes such a pill, this one purchased from the black market. Unfortunately, rather than sending blood to that location, they find themselves with engorged hands.*

980. *An unnamed character takes a pill to help with a small ailment. Throughout the day they feel random bursts of hot flashes merged with cold sweats. By the end of it, they have become the opposite gender.*

981.   *Envision the above scenario, but rather than becoming the opposite gender, the individual becomes a new one entirely. For a variation, they lose the physicality that comes with gender. How might their perception of reality change now?*

982.   *A young teen visits a friend's house for dinner. The friend is adamant that it's not a good idea, but the teen is persistent. After all, their friend has come over for dinner several times. When dinner is served, it isn't like anything the teen has ever eaten. Rather than be rude, they manage to get the strange goop down. As soon as they finish, their stomach begins to churn and they double over in pain. That's when the first round of changes start.*

983.   *A botched plastic surgery renders an individual horribly disfigured. Previous to this surgery, they were voted one of the most beautiful on Earth. Now they must deal with children that scream when they approach and adults that try to avoid eye contact.*

984.   *Scientists are calling it "The Medusa" syndrome. It begins to occur when a new shampoo hits the market and causes hair to become rope-like, akin to the appearance of snakes. For one poor individual, their hair actually does become slithering serpents. They must have gotten a really bad batch!*

985.   *A new fertility drug hits the market, but it comes with a dire warning: Under no circumstances should men take this product. A young couple trying to conceive a baby buys the new medicine. Due to an unforeseen mix-up, the man*

inadvertently becomes the first biological male to become pregnant.

986. *A farmer has a side hobby: wannabe scientist. They have spent months working on a replicator that will boost up their animal stock. However, an accident causes them to inadvertently use the machine on themselves, but not before one of the animals gets in the way. Rather than making two sets--two farmers and two animals—the species merge.*

987. *During a heavy rainstorm, a group of homeless individuals unknowingly wander into a laboratory for shelter. One of them accidentally walks into a weather testing machine and becomes part of the weather.*

988. *An unnamed character has a habit of wearing plastic animal masks to take photos with. During a lightning storm, they are struck while taking a selfie. When they go to remove the mask, they can't. It's been fused to their skin. Now they must live life with an animal head and human body.*

989. *A shrink ray is finally invented. Only the elite can experience life from a 2-inch view. As a result, a group of individuals hijack the ray and alter it. The next time it is used, the paying individuals stay small.*

990. *Imagine a similar scenario, but individuals do not willingly use the shrink ray. In fact, the company that makes the ray has been rounding up individuals and forcing them to fight insects in a makeshift tiny Coliseum. Not only do they allow*

the rich to view these battles on monitors, but they can also place bets.

991. *A new disorder is discovered. It is prominently known as "Alice Syndrome". Although only one case has been found so far, it is notable for causing the individual to shrink to the size of a small bug.*

992. *Imagine this syndrome doesn't cause an individual to get smaller, but bigger—much, much bigger. For a variation, envision a scenario in which the individual cannot stop growing at a rapid pace.*

993. *Obsessed with horror culture, a scientist tries to create the world's first werewolf by experimenting on himself. Fortunately, the serum he creates works well. Unfortunately, the sample he uses isn't a wolf like he thought. It's a Chihuahua. For a variation, use any breed of dog, or even another animal.*

994. *A scientist, deeply burdened by the tragic loss of their family at a young age, sets about making a traditional nuclear family to replace them. Dead bodies do not work and they cannot go out and kidnap people. So they turn to the next best thing: a group of teenagers who get lost on their way to a concert. The scientist decides to drug them and use surgery to give them new faces and bodies.*

995. *An unnamed character becomes obsessed with their favorite celebrity. So much so, they pay an affluent plastic surgeon to make them look exactly like them.*

Unfortunately, the surgeon has other plans and is dying to try out a new "look".

996. *An unnamed character takes some medication to help with their social anxiety. It does what it is intended to do, but in an exaggerated facet. They become so personable, everyone is instantly drawn to them. As a result, they can get whatever they want—at least, for the few hours the medicine is effective.*

997. *A new serum is invented that allows workers of hazardous sites to forgo the use of safety equipment because their bodies adapt to the dangers. For instance, if the individual is a window washer, then their body might have some degree of anti-gravity. Or if they are working near an active volcano, then their body might develop rocky, craggy skin. Craft a narrative in which the first test subject is put through a series of rigorous tests to see how well the serum works.*

998. *A scientist is working on a series of tests that are meant to determine how mental changes lead to physical ones. They are supposed to only make the subject believe they are under nonexistent pain to see how their body adapts. However, the scientist accidentally mixes up the viewing disc and plays an old monster movie that is from the perspective of the monster. As a result, the subject believes there are torch wielding townspeople chasing them. Curiously, their skin takes on a few shades of green.*

999.   While undergoing surgery, an unlikeable character is being discussed by the gathered surgeons. They could easily remove the tumors and be done with it, but the character is such a jerk they decide to teach them a lesson. They give them a tail.

1000.   The paper promises $250 for a few minutes of time. An unnamed character, down on their luck, can't resist. When they arrive at the lab, they are told some changes might occur, but if all goes well they will double their payment by the end of the experiment. The character decides to go for it. True to their world, the scientists pays out $500. The problem is, the character has been turned into a monster.

1001.   An unnamed character knows they do not have much longer to live and sets about trying to escape death by creating a machine that will help them sustain their life. The goal is to create a robot body. But something goes wrong. Instead of implanting their conscious in the robot body, it is implanted in the TV. For a variation, this conscious can be put into any random electrical device.

ABOUT THE AUTHOR

Christina Escamilla is an author, illustrator, and lover of all things books. When she doesn't have her nose stuck in one, she can be found watching a documentary about theoretical science or exploring the vast reaches of the Internet.

To learn more about her visit:

www.stinaesc.com

Made in the USA
Coppell, TX
26 April 2025

48733337R00128